Journey
of Faith

Journey of Faith

DAILY DEVOTIONS

Candace Brown Doud

XULON PRESS

Xulon Press
2301 Lucien Way #415
Maitland, FL 32751
407.339.4217
www.xulonpress.com

Unless otherwise indicated, Scripture quotations taken from the Holy Bible, New International Version (NIV). Copyright © 1973, 1978, 1984, 2011 by Biblica, Inc.™. Used by permission. All rights reserved.

Printed in the United States of America

Paperback ISBN-13: 9781662800696
Hard Cover ISBN-13: 9781662800702
Ebook ISBN-13: 9781662800719

To my family, with all my love,
as we continue our own journey of faith.

DEAR READER,

O ur world may seem like it is spiraling out of control, but don't worry, it's not. God is on His Throne and very much in control. He made this earth just for us, and His purposes will never be thwarted. We can trust Him with our life and our future.

Journey of Faith is written to help us relinquish our fears and insecurities to Him. Monthly themes with daily verses from Genesis to Revelation, along with personal application and a closing prayer, will be our guide, as we focus on our never-changing God in a constantly changing world—until Jesus returns! Enjoy the journey!

Candace Brown Doud
September 2020

MONTHLY THEMES

Faith

Love

Fear

Truth

Hope

Strength

Joy

Grace

Mercy

Holiness

Prayer

Peace

January

FAITH

❧

Our journey begins with **faith**.
How do we build up our faith along the way?

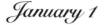

BE SURE

*Now **faith** is being sure of what we hope for and
certain of what we do not see.*
Hebrews 11:1

What is faith? We can define faith as complete trust in someone or something. We can have faith in all kinds of things—the lifeguard guarding us, the doctor treating us, the teacher teaching us, the church, the stock market, the government, even ourselves. But there are no guarantees in that kind of faith because it is not biblical faith. Biblical faith is not based on what others do for us, or we can do for ourselves, but on everything God has done for us and history has proven. *We can be sure of what we hope for and certain of what we do not see,* because of what Jesus Christ did for us on the cross.

As we begin our journey of faith, and work our way through the Bible each month, let's be sure our faith is in Him. I guarantee He will make our faith stronger along the way.

Whom or what is your faith in other than the saving faith of Jesus Christ?

PRAYER

Lord Jesus, help me put my total trust in You as the only One who can save me from my sin.

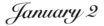

SOLID GROUND

*If you do not stand firm in your **faith**,*
you will not stand at all.
Isaiah 7:9

Everyone believes in something, and what we believe determines how we live. To put it another way, we behave the way we behave, because we believe what we believe. When we believe that God sent His Son into the world to save us from sin, we are free of the bondage, the guilt, the punishment, and the penalty our sin deserves. Jesus took our sins upon Himself and they were nailed to the cross on Calvary. We are free to live the life God created us to live.

Jesus gives us the strength to stand strong in a world that is constantly pulling us down. To quote a popular hymn, "all other ground is sinking sand!" Get on solid ground with Jesus.

Are you standing on solid ground with Jesus?

PRAYER

Lord Jesus, put my feet on solid ground with You so I can grow in my journey of faith.

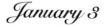

BE RIGHT! CHOOSE FAITH

*See, he is puffed up; his desires are not upright – but
the righteous will live by his* **faith**.
Habakkuk 2:4

The Old Testament prophet Habakkuk spoke these words thousands of years ago to the people of Judah to draw a contrast between those who live for themselves and those who live for God. Every generation in every nation has lived with the same conflict. Either we trust ourselves and our own resources or we trust God and depend on His.

Like many people today, Habakkuk wondered why God allowed people to prosper without Him. Both choices require faith, but I'd rather put my faith in the eternal God of the universe than myself. How about you?

Are you tired of doing life alone? If so, Jesus is waiting. Give yourself a break and put your trust in Him and see where He takes you in the new year.

PRAYER

Lord Jesus, I am tired of doing life alone. Help me put my faith in You and watch expectantly for what You will do this year.

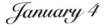

HOW MUCH FAITH?

*If that is how God clothes the grass of the field, which is here today and tomorrow is thrown into the fire, will he not much more clothe you, O you of little **faith**?*
Matthew 6:30

These words are from Jesus' own lips. He turned the world upside down with His teaching. People worried then just as they do today, and worry and faith are incompatible. Worry leads us away from God. Faith leads us to Him.

Jesus is teaching His followers then and now to trust Him with our needs. After all, if He created this earth with all its beauty and sustains it for our use and enjoyment, who are we to doubt that He will care for us. Let's don't be people of little faith. Let's ask Him for more.

How much are you trusting Jesus for your needs?

PRAYER

Lord Jesus, I cannot worry and trust You at the same time. Increase my faith so I trust You more.

FAITH OVER FEAR

*He said to his disciples, "Why are you so afraid? Do you still have no **faith**?"*
Mark 4:40

Faith and fear have always been at odds with one another. In this passage in Mark, the disciples and Jesus were in a boat on the Sea of Galilee when a huge storm came up threatening their survival. The disciples were terrified, while Jesus was asleep. Two different reactions to the same circumstances. Jesus was teaching them—and He is teaching us what most of us know—life is uncertain, and storms are inevitable. But in every situation we face and every storm we go through, He is with us. Sometimes it may seem like He is sleeping, but it's far better to be in the boat with Him than to be in the boat alone.

How are you allowing fear to squelch your faith today?

PRAYER

Lord Jesus, please help my trust in You overcome the needless fears I create.

January 6

GROW YOUR FAITH

*The apostles said to the Lord,
"Increase our **faith**!"*
Luke 17:5

Do you ever wonder why you don't have more faith, or wonder how you could, or envy people that do? Jesus' earthly ministry was devoted to teaching His followers to believe in Him as the long-awaited Messiah. He built faith into them, so they could carry on after Him. His answer to the disciples that day still astounds us. He said, "If you have faith as small as a mustard seed, you can say to this mulberry tree, 'Be uprooted and planted in the sea,' and it will obey you . . . ." Jesus used this tiny, familiar seed to encourage His followers not to be discouraged if their faith seemed small, but to nurture it. After all, when our faith is in Jesus that tiny seed could someday grow into a tree.

How much faith do you want to have and what are you doing to make it grow?

PRAYER

Lord Jesus, help me want to know Your teachings in Your Word so my faith in You grows.

SET APART

I am sending you to them to open their eyes and turn them from darkness to light, and from the power of Satan to God, so that they may receive forgiveness of sins and a place among those who are sanctified by **faith** *in me.*
Acts 26:17-18

When we come to faith in Jesus Christ, we are set apart from the world and set apart for Him. His Holy Spirit moves into us and begins a process called Sanctification that is designed to make us more like Jesus. It requires our cooperation and continues until we die and see Him face to face. In the meantime, we have the privilege of joining His rescue mission of leading people like ourselves out of the darkness and into the light. Don't miss being set apart from the world and set apart for Him. It's the best!

Are you willing to be set apart from the world so God can set you apart for Him?

PRAYER

Lord Jesus, help me want to be set apart *from* the world so You can use me *in* the world.

BREAKING NEWS

I thank my God through Jesus Christ for all of you,
*because your **faith** is being reported all over the world.*
Romans 1:8

What are you known for? What do people think of when they think of you? What about you has the most effect on the people in your world? We can be remembered for lots of things, but the only lasting memory that will most impact lives now, and the generations that follow, is our faith and trust in Jesus Christ.

My maternal grandmother left me with the beautiful memory of Bible verses posted around her house. I remember seeing her get up in the morning and immediately drop to her knees to start her day with Him. Like her, I want to be remembered as a woman of faith, because in the end nothing else matters. Share the Breaking News—His good news.

What do you want to be remembered for?

PRAYER

Lord Jesus, help me be a person of faith so people think of You when they think of me.

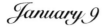

NOT GUILTY!

*For we maintain that a man is justified by **faith** apart
from observing the law.*
Romans 3:28

In God's Court of Law, we are all sinners condemned to physical death in this life and eternal death in the next, because we have failed to keep His law, which for us is basically the Ten Commandments. No one can claim innocence because no one has kept them all perfectly every minute of every day of their life. Therefore, we all stand condemned. But Jesus stood in our place, took the punishment we deserve, and when we put our faith in Him, we can stand before God forgiven. And the verdict for all of Heaven to hear is, "Not guilty!"

Have you come to Jesus for forgiveness, so you can stand before God and hear those amazing words?

PRAYER

Lord Jesus, help me see myself as a sinner in need of Your forgiveness. I yearn to be set free. Thank You for taking the punishment I deserve so I am.

CREDIT YOUR ACCOUNT

*To the man who does not work but trusts God who justifies the wicked, his **faith** is credited as righteousness.*
Romans 4:5

Paul uses a banking analogy to explain faith. He makes it clear that God doesn't credit our faith account with the works or good deeds we do, but with the faith we have. That puts faith on a level playing field. We can all have it—as much as we want. And yet we are constantly trying to make ourselves righteous. The self-help books that fill our bookstores prove it. We want to be better people for our families, our careers, and hopefully God. The problem is, we can never be good enough or do good enough to enter God's holy Heaven. He made sure of it. That's where faith comes in, and we can have as much of that as we want. Credit your account.

Are you still trying to make yourself right before God, when what He wants is your faith?

PRAYER

Lord Jesus, forgive me for thinking I can somehow make myself right before You. Change my thinking and my heart. Credit my faith account with more faith in You.

THE BOTTOM LINE

*"The word is near you; it is in your mouth and in your heart," that is, the word of **faith** we are proclaiming: That if you confess with your mouth, "Jesus is Lord," and believe in your heart that God raised him from the dead, you will be saved.*
Romans 10:8-9

Our salvation was costly to God—it cost Him His Son. It was costly to Jesus—it cost Him His life. But salvation is free for us to accept. It is ours for the taking. It is the greatest gift we will ever receive. But we must accept it by believing in our heart and confessing with our mouth Jesus is Lord and that God raised Him from the dead.

When my father was dying, he called me to him and asked me what he had to do to be right with God. Being the businessman he was, he said, "Candy, just give me the bottom line." I said, "Daddy, God loves you, Jesus died for you, and He wants you to come to Him. Confess your sins and commit your life to Him—that's the bottom line." Thank God, he did.

Have you responded to this "word of faith?" If not, don't wait until you are dying. Do it now, while you can.

PRAYER

Lord Jesus, please open my heart to receive You and my mouth to confess You.

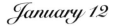

LISTEN UP!

Faith *comes from hearing the message, and the message is heard through the word of Christ.*
Romans 10:17

We can't have faith in God, apart from the Word of God, simply because we can't know Him without it. The two are intertwined and inseparable. We are all exposed to His Word at some time and to some degree no matter how minimal. The problem is not with our exposure, but with our response. Our response to God and to His Word are our responsibility. Unfortunately, we live in a world that is increasingly hostile to anything relating to God, Jesus, or the Bible. Yet the Bible remains the one absolute for every generation to turn to and follow. It contains everything we need to know for this life and the next. We better listen up!

How important is the Bible to you?

PRAYER

Lord Jesus, I want to grow in my faith. Please give me a compelling desire to study Your Word so I can continue my journey of faith.

USE IT UP!

*We have different gifts, according to the grace given us. If a man's gift is prophesying, let him use it in proportion to his **faith**. If it is serving, let him serve; if it is teaching, let him teach; if it is encouraging, let him encourage; if it is contributing to the needs of others, let him give generously; if it is leadership, let him govern diligently; if it is showing mercy, let him do it cheerfully.*
Romans 12:6-9

God has given every believer certain gifts to be used within His Church, the body of believers around the world. He wants us to maximize these gifts, both for our benefit and those we serve. We grow stronger in our faith when we recognize and share our gifts with one another. So what's the point in holding back? Let's not be afraid to use up what we've been given, because there's always more where that came from.

How are you making the most of the gifts God has given you for His Kingdom?

PRAYER

Lord Jesus, please help me use the gifts You have given me. Help me use them up for You.

January 14

DON'T FLAUNT IT

*Don't flaunt your **faith** in front of others who might be hurt by it.*
Romans 14:22 (TLB)

God hates spiritual pride. He never wants us to show off our faith or flaunt it in a prideful way that makes others feel inferior, inadequate, or insecure. He wants our faith to be a magnet that draws others to Him, so He can strengthen their faith. That can only happen when we are sensitive to our company, our surroundings, and His Holy Spirit in us. He will guide us to encourage their faith and not hinder it. Sometimes that means, for example, giving up a glass of wine because it's a problem for the person we're with. We miss God's blessing when we flaunt our faith in a prideful way.

Does your faith in Jesus draw others to Him or push them away?

PRAYER

Lord Jesus, help me never flaunt my faith. Instead, help me be grateful and let my faith be a magnet, drawing others to You.

STAND FIRM

*Be on your guard; stand firm in the **faith**; be men of courage; be strong.*
1 Corinthians 16:13

We live in the world of "anything goes." A world of no moral absolutes. A world that is turning away from the truth of God's Word and turning to the lies Satan promotes. The closer we move toward Jesus' return, the more this trend will continue, because Satan's time is running out. It's time for us to dig deep, to know what we believe and why, to guard our faith and be ready to defend it, to stand firm and not let anything or anyone dissuade us, to be courageous instead of complacent and strong instead of weak. We must stand firm for Jesus, because He did the same for us. As His followers, how can we do less?

How are you standing firm in your faith, and where do you need to be stronger?

PRAYER

Lord Jesus, help me stand firm in my faith so people know where I stand and are drawn to You as well.

BLIND FAITH

*For we live by **faith**, not by sight.*
2 Corinthians 5:7

A s a sighted person, it's hard to imagine navigating through life totally blind. Confidence and trust would be the only way to navigate and survive in a sight-dependent world.

Likewise, confidence and trust in Jesus Christ and His Word is the navigational guide believers depend on. Our physical sight can lead us astray as we observe what is happening in our world. We can become caught up in wrong thinking, anxiety, frustration, and fear that has become the norm. We can allow the world to dictate our actions instead of depending on our faith to guide us. It requires determination to stay in God's Word and let Him lead us. But oh, the blessings when we do!

What GPS system are you using to navigate through life right now, yours or God's?

PRAYER

Lord Jesus, help me stop trusting myself and put my confidence and trust in You.

I SURRENDER!

*I have been crucified with Christ
and I no longer live, but Christ lives in me. The life I
live in the body, I live by **faith** in the Son of God, who
loved me and gave himself for me.*
Galatians 2:20

If Jesus Christ came to this earth as God in the flesh and died for my sins—as though I was the only person on this planet—because He loved me too much not to, what can I do but surrender my life to Him? And if His Holy Spirit chooses to live in me and provide me with all the love, knowledge, wisdom, companionship, guidance, strength, grace, and protection I can possibly contain, how can I not trust Him with my life now and my death whenever and however it comes? When we live by faith in Christ, we are free to live the life He created us to live, and we die in the peace of that reality.

Have you totally surrendered your life to Jesus, or are you living on the fringes of your faith in Him? Make this the day you give it all to Him.

PRAYER

Lord Jesus, help me totally surrender my life to You today.

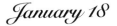

FREE IN JESUS
---

*Now that **faith** has come, we are no longer under the supervision of the law.*
Galatians 3:25

G od's law kept the Israelites in line and taught them about Him and what He expected of them. The law was like a tutor preparing them to receive Jesus Christ who fulfilled or satisfied the law with His perfect life. The law is summarized for us in the Ten Commandments. They lead us to Christ, because they show us how we fail to keep them and therefore how much we need Him. Without Jesus taking our punishment, we are subject to eternal separation from God. Thank God for Jesus. In Him, we are free of the judgment our sin deserves.

Do you know the Ten Commandments, so you are aware of your inability to keep them and your need for Jesus to set you free?

PRAYER

Lord Jesus, thank You for forgiving me and taking the punishment I deserve.

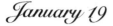

THE FAMILY OF GOD

*As opportunity offers, let us work
for the good of all, especially members
of the household of **faith**.*
Galatians 6:10 (NET)

God has given us a great gift in the Church, the body of believers around the world. We are there for each other no matter the denomination or which church we attend. We are family, and we look out for, care for, and pray for each other. We work together for the common goal of building our faith and sharing it with others. We are Christ's ambassadors to spread the gospel, the good news about Him, so others can believe as well. He wants everyone who will, to come and be part of the family. Nothing makes His family of believers more appealing than watching them care for their own. God's family is the best family.

What good work can you do for someone in the family and someone not yet in the family?

PRAYER

Lord Jesus, show me whom I can reach out to for You today.

BOAST ABOUT JESUS

For it is by grace you have been saved, through
faith—*and this not from yourselves, it is the gift of*
God—not by works, so that no one can boast.
Ephesians 2:8-9

God makes it clear that our salvation has nothing to do with what we do, but everything to do with what He did. We cannot buy, bribe, or force our way into Heaven. Only His grace, or undeserved favor toward us, makes it possible. This eliminates tooting our own horn when we get there. As prideful as we are, we would arrive with a list of deeds and accomplishments that merit our presence. But Heaven is His Home, and He is on the Throne. We will be so overjoyed and grateful to be in His presence that anything we did on earth will pale in comparison, insignificant to His magnificence. Let's boast about Him instead of ourselves.

How are you boasting about God for what He has done for you instead of boasting about yourself and what you have done for Him?

PRAYER

Lord Jesus, You have done it all. Help me boast about You instead of myself.

CHOOSE YOUR IDENTITY

*One Lord, one **faith**, one baptism.*
Ephesians 4:5

I dentity is important to all of us. We need to know who we are, why we are here, and who is going to be there for us. We are all identified with someone or something in this life—some person, family, career, organization, education, or achievement.

Baptism is the act by which we identify with Jesus. He set the example for us. His baptism announced His Messiahship, began His public ministry, and identified Him as God's Son. Even though He was without sin, He chose to be baptized to show us the way. There is only one Lord, one Faith, and one Baptism. Baptism links us with Him. Choose your identity.

Have you publicly identified yourself with Jesus? Do people know you are?

PRAYER

Lord Jesus, help me claim my identity in You and be bold to make it known.

DON'T FORGET YOUR SHIELD

*Take up the shield of **faith**, with which you can
extinguish all the flaming arrows of the evil one.*
Ephesians 6:16

This world is a war zone—a war between the forces of good and the forces of evil. God is the source of all that is good; Satan is the source of all that is evil. And in the end, God wins! But in the meantime, the wicked one loves to attack us any way he can. Our only defense against his fiery darts of accusation, anxiety, discouragement, guilt, fear, insecurity, hopelessness, and despair—just to name some of his favorites—is the shield of faith. Nothing can penetrate it, because nothing can separate us from the love of God. He proved it on the cross. Satan is a defeated foe. Don't forget your shield.

Are you allowing Satan to get you down? Don't stay there. Put your shield of faith on and get up!

PRAYER

Lord Jesus, thank You for the shield of faith. Help me not to leave home without it.

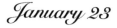

✑

DELIVER US FROM EVIL

*And pray that we may be
delivered from wicked and evil men,
for not everyone has **faith**.*
2 Thessalonians 3:2

Without faith in God, we are separated from Him. We are aimlessly wandering through life on our own. We are cut off from His divine purpose with no compass and no connection to His will for our lives. In this separated state, God considers us unreasonable and wicked, because we have rejected Him, when all He wants for us is good. He has blessed us with the free will to choose our path in life but there are only two. Either we choose Him and go His way, or by default we choose Satan and go his way. People question why there is so much evil in the world, and the answer is clear: people make the wrong choice. Be delivered. Choose God.

Are you counted among those of faith?

PRAYER

Lord Jesus, deliver me from evil and help me be counted among those of faith.

January 24

✣

BELIEVERS, BEWARE!

*The Spirit clearly says that in later times some will
abandon the **faith**
and follow deceiving spirits and
things taught by demons.*
1 Timothy 4:1

Most Bible scholars agree we could be living in the end times. Jesus said we can't know the day or the hour of His return, but we can read the signs. Today there are many—beginning with Israel becoming a state in 1948 and from then—increasing wars, natural disasters, terrorism, famines, pestilence, godlessness, break-down in families, loss of respect for authority, lawlessness, and a falling away from the faith. Our screens keep us posted of the next calamity. Our stress levels have never been higher. It's obvious, Satan is having a heyday, because he knows his time is running out and Jesus' return is imminent. Believers, beware! Don't be deceived! Guard the faith!

Is your faith in Christ solid enough to withstand these end time assaults from the enemy? If not, now is the time to shore it up.

PRAYER

Lord Jesus, help me shore up my faith through Your Word, so I am not deceived by the enemy.

January 25

FINISH STRONG

I have fought the good fight, I have finished the race,
*I have kept the **faith**.*
2 Timothy 4:7

Life is hard. Satan makes sure of it. He and his demon friends constantly try to take us down, discourage us, and keep us from keeping the faith. Satan wants us to finish the race of life without making an impact on others and without leaving a legacy of faith to our children and grandchildren. He wants our faith to waver as we get older. He wants us to die without much attention. He certainly doesn't want to see a Celebration of Life Memorial Service with Jesus as the Guest of Honor, and people having their faith strengthened because of ours. Let's foil Satan's plans. Let's fight to the end and finish the race with our faith stronger than ever before.

Where are you in your life of faith in Jesus Christ? Where do you want to be at the end of your life?

PRAYER

Lord Jesus, help me fight the fight and finish my race strong in You!

CLAIM YOUR REWARD

*And without **faith** it is impossible to please God,
because anyone who comes to him must believe that
he exists and that he rewards those who earnestly
seek him.*
Hebrews 11:6

God takes our faith seriously, because what we believe determines how we behave. Only when we believe He is who He says He is will our life be transformed. Believing in Him gives Him permission to guide us into becoming the person He created us to be. It is the first step of a life-long journey with Him. Our worldview changes, our attitudes change, our priorities change, our ambitions and desires change, our outlook on life changes, and our hope for the future changes. He rewards us with His companionship through His Holy Spirit now and the security of knowing we will be with Him forever. Live to please God and claim your reward.

Is your faith pleasing to God, because you take Him seriously and live like you do?

PRAYER

Lord Jesus, I want to please You. Help me take my faith seriously and live like I do.

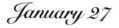

TAKE THE RISK

*By **faith** the prostitute Rahab, because she welcomed the spies, was not killed with those who were disobedient.*
Hebrews 11:31

F aith always involves taking a risk; otherwise it wouldn't be faith. Rahab is a perfect example. She lived in the land God had promised the Israelites. When they were about to take over, she hid some of their spies and then lied to her own people to protect them. Rahab had heard of Israel's God and took the risk and aligned with Him. God rewarded her not only by sparing her life, but also by listing her, a former prostitute, in the genealogy of His Son.

God wants us to know that nothing in our background can keep us from Him, when we come, like Rahab did, and want to follow Him. When we do, a whole new life awaits us. Take the risk.

What risk are you willing to take for Jesus?

PRAYER

Lord Jesus, help me be willing to take a risk for You because I trust You.

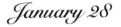

BE CAREFUL WHAT YOU WANT

Listen, my dear brothers:
Has not God chosen those who are poor in the eyes
*of the world to be rich in **faith** and to inherit the*
kingdom he promised to those who love him?
James 2:5

My brother was rich in the eyes of the world but poor in the eyes of God. God used a poor man in the eyes of the world to make him rich in His eyes. A plumber working on his beautiful house left a gospel tract on his toilet. My brother took it. Later, in the pouring down rain with tears pouring down his face, he read it and became rich.

God has nothing against being rich—Abraham was very rich—but God is a jealous God and wants us to love Him more, trust Him more, and need Him more than anything material. He knows those things might give us temporary pleasure, but being rich in Him brings eternal pleasure. Be careful what you want.

How determined are you to have the riches of God over the riches of this world?

PRAYER

Lord Jesus, help me to want more of You and less of this world.

GENUINE FAITH

What good is it, my brothers, if a man claims to have
faith *but has no deeds? Can such* ***faith*** *save him?*
James 2:14

W hen we say we believe something but live like we don't, we are hypocrites. We are living a lie. We are fake news. If our faith in Jesus Christ is genuine, our life will reflect it, because it will affect everything we do. Faith in Him will dictate our thoughts, words, and actions. We will stand out in a world that wants us to blend in. We will serve Christ in the way we live, because our love for Him will not allow otherwise. If, on the other hand, we profess to believe in Him but nothing in our life backs that up, we are misleading ourselves and those around us. Let's check our faith and make sure our life reflects it. That's genuine faith.

Are people seeing that your faith is genuine because of the way you live?

PRAYER

Lord Jesus, help my life reflect that my faith is genuine.

January 30

BUILD ON YOUR FOUNDATION

*Make every effort to add to your **faith** goodness; and to goodness, knowledge; and to knowledge, self-control; and to self-control, perseverance; and to perseverance, godliness; and to godliness, brotherly kindness; and to brotherly kindness, love.*
2 Peter 1:5-7

F aith in Jesus Christ is the foundation stone for building a godly character. It begins His transforming work in our lives. His goal is to make us more and more like Him. Hence the name Christian. We are to grow more and more like Christ as we journey through life.

Faith, goodness, knowledge, self-control, perseverance, godliness, brotherly kindness, and love are godly virtues. These virtues are more necessary than ever in our fast-paced, self-centered, and godless society. These virtues set us apart and draw others to Him. We are to make every effort to know them, cultivate them, and show them to the world. Build on your foundation.

Which of these virtues reflects your life, and which ones do you need to work on?

PRAYER

Lord Jesus, help me make every effort to be more and more like You.

CLAIM THE VICTORY

*This is the victory that has overcome
the world, even our **faith**.*
1 John 5:4

When we give our lives to Jesus Christ, we immediately leave the kingdom of this world and enter the kingdom of God. We become members of His family. His Holy Spirit comes into us to help us live life the way God wants us to. He becomes our Counselor and Guide to lead us in the way we should go. He warns us when we are about to sin and convicts us when we do.

All of God's resources are available to help us break from our past way of living and embrace the new. We have the power in us to overcome anything the enemy throws our way. We can live in the victory Jesus won for us on the cross.

Are you living in this victory, or are you still allowing the world to keep you from it?

PRAYER

Lord Jesus, thank You for my faith in You that gives me the power to live in victory instead of defeat.

February

LOVE

❧

Let's learn about **love**—God's love for us and our love
for others—on our journey of faith.

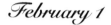

February 1

$\mathcal{D}\!\!\mathcal{O}$

GO TO THE SOURCE

*God is **love**.*
1 John 4:16

Today the word love is used so casually that we can miss its true meaning and significance. But God sets the standard of love because He is love. Love is intrinsic to Him, because it's His nature to love. As believers, it must become our nature as well. We must differentiate the world's type of love, which loves burgers and fries, from God's love, which loved us "before the foundation of the world." We must know the difference and take love seriously, because He takes it seriously. Our love must align with His love. This is the perfect month and the perfect verse to begin our study of love in His Word. As we continue our journey of faith, let's go to the Source.

Do you know the love of God in your own life? Are you excited to learn how you can more fully understand His love so you can love like He does?

PRAYER

Lord Jesus, the world's definition of love is different than Yours. Help me learn to love like You do.

February 2

ALL IN!

*You shall **love** the Lord your God
with all heart and with all your soul
and with all your strength.*
Deuteronomy 6:5

God commands us to love Him. It is not a suggestion or a good idea, but a command, His first and most important command. His love initiates our relationship with Him. We cannot love Him without Him first loving us. And we can't love Him in return without knowing He loves us.

God is specific in the way we are to love Him. We are to love Him with all our heart because our heart is the seat of our emotions, with all our soul because our soul is the very core of us, and with all our strength because He wants us to be all in for Him. God wants to be first in our life, and He doesn't want to share that position with anyone or anything else. Let's be all in for Jesus.

Is God first in your life? If not, will you allow Him to be?

PRAYER

Lord Jesus, help me put You first in my life and love You the way You deserve to be loved—with all that I am.

February 3

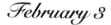

BE A SAINT

Love *the Lord, all his saints! The Lord preserves the
faithful, but the proud
he pays back in full.*
Psalm 31:23

The Bible often refers to believers as saints. We are His beloved! Therefore, just as Jesus demonstrated His love for us on the cross, we are to demonstrate our love for Him in return. It's not enough just to say we love Him; we have to live like we do. We have to prove it by being humble, grateful, faithful, consistent, and intentional. Just as He proved His love for us on the cross, we must prove our love for Him in the choices we make. Our love for Him must become the driving force in our life and motivate our worship, thanksgiving, desires, attitudes, and service. It's a privilege to be a saint.

How will you demonstrate your love for Jesus in a specific way today?

PRAYER

Lord Jesus, help me demonstrate Your love in a specific way to someone today.

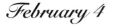

UNDER HIS UMBRELLA

*"Because he **loves** me," says the Lord, "I will rescue him; I will protect him, for he acknowledges my name. He will call upon me, and I will answer him; I will be with him in trouble, I will deliver him and honor him. With long life will I satisfy him and show him my salvation."*
Psalm 91:14-16

In this world of uncertainty and insecurity, is there any greater promise than to be under the umbrella of God's love? He loves each one of us as His unique creation, but He waits for our love in return to complete the relationship. When we align ourselves with Him, we become His adopted sons and daughters, and as such, we can trust Him because we are under His protection and sovereign care. We are under His umbrella.

Are you under the umbrella of God's love because you have chosen to love Him in return? If not, now is the perfect time. Tell Him you love Him and accept His offer of forgiveness through His Son Jesus Christ. Then commit your life to Him going forward.

PRAYER

Lord Jesus, thank You for putting me under the umbrella of Your love.

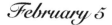

February 5

GOD'S GPS SYSTEM

*Oh, how I **love** your law!*
I meditate on it all day long.
Psalm 119:97

God gave the Israelites His law to live by so they would survive, and to make them into the people He wanted them to be. Today we have the Bible, His written Word, to help us do the same. The Bible is our source of truth and wisdom. It is our manual for living. It is our compass, our navigational aid, our own GPS system. It is the only absolute we can turn to in a world that is losing its way.

As believers in Jesus Christ, we are to read, study, and know His Word because we love Him, and we are to let it saturate our hearts and minds, so it directs everything we do. Let His GPS guide you.

How much time and effort do you give God's Word each day so He can guide you?

PRAYER

Lord Jesus, help me to make it a daily priority to study Your Word so You can guide my life.

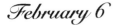

February 6

THAT'S LOVE

But I tell you: **Love** *your enemies and pray for those
who persecute you.*
Matthew 5:44

It's easy to love people who love us, think like us, and treat us with kindness and respect. Jesus didn't wait for people to love Him. The hallmark of His ministry was His unconditional love. He didn't agree with everyone or approve of their actions or accept them in His tight circle. He openly exposed the religious leaders for their hypocrisy and called sin, sin. And He only chose twelve men to be His first disciples. But He loved everyone, and He proved it by praying for them, and for us, even while experiencing the most brutal death ever on the cross. He prayed, "Father, forgive them, for they do not know what they are doing" (Luke 23:34). That's love.

How can you show Jesus' love and pray for your enemies, like He did?

PRAYER

Lord Jesus, help me love like You do. Help me pray for my enemies like You did.

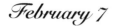

February 7

THE GREATEST NEWS

*For God so **loved** the world that he
gave his one and only Son, that whoever believes in
him shall not perish but
have eternal life.*
John 3:16

This verse is probably the most well-known verse in the Bible. Churches teach it, children memorize it, and it's posted on social media in hundreds of languages all over the world. It contains the very essence of the gospel—the good news that Jesus Christ came to this earth to die for our sins so we could have everlasting life. It is the crux of our Christian faith and becomes the defining moment in our life as soon as we read it or hear it. This verse lays the foundation for our understanding of love. God's love motivated Him to send Jesus to die for us so we could spend eternity with Him. Is there any greater love than that? No! It's the greatest news of all time.

Are you included in the "whoever believes"? Today is the day to make sure you are.

PRAYER

Lord Jesus, help me accept this greatest news for myself and then pass it on to someone else.

February 8

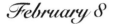

GUARD YOUR HEART

*But I know you. I know that you do not have the **love***
of God in your hearts.
John 5:42

There is a difference between knowing about Jesus and knowing Jesus. Intellectual knowledge is different than heart knowledge. Approximately eighteen inches separates our head from our heart, but that can mean the difference between going to Heaven and going to Hell. Jesus wants our heart because that is where love dwells, and He wants our love more than just our mind's acknowledgment or assent. When we truly love Him, our lives will reflect His love, and we will be a valuable witness to His work in this world. People will meet His love when they meet us, which is all the more reason to guard our hearts. He lives there and He wants people to know it. Guard your heart.

What are you doing to guard your heart from loving something or someone else more than you love Jesus?

PRAYER

Lord Jesus, help me guard my heart from loving anyone or anything more than I love You.

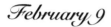

THE BEST LIFE

*The man who **loves** his life will lose it,*
while the man who hates his life in this world will keep
it for eternal life.
John 12:25

Whehen we love Jesus more than we love life here on earth, we are leaving something of life behind. We are making a statement that we would rather have Jesus than anything the world offers. We are saying we value eternal life more than this life, which is temporary and fleeting. We are saying that we are actually foreigners here and our permanent residence is Heaven. The world doesn't understand this kind of thinking, and it's our great privilege as believers to make it appealing so they will. Choose the best life!

Are you loving this life so much that you have little time to think about the next life?

PRAYER

Lord Jesus, help me make the right choices here so I am prepared to live with You in Heaven.

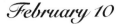

THE ULTIMATE LOVE

*Having **loved** his own who were*
in the world, he now showed them
*the full extent of his **love**.*
John 13:1

The night before Jesus died, the night of His Last Supper with His friends on this earth, He left us with this indelible memory. Because of the dusty roads and the fact that the men wore sandals, it was customary for a slave to wash their feet. But this was a special night. Jesus became the 'slave' and washed the disciple's feet. Think of it! God Incarnate, who left the glory of Heaven, loving them enough to come down here and wash their feet—and if we had been there that night, He would have washed ours too! It's hard for us to conceive of such love, but God's love puts others first. God's love is the ultimate love.

To whom can you show that kind of self-sacrificing love today?

PRAYER

Lord Jesus, show me whom I can love with Your self-sacrificing love today.

SHOW IT OFF

By this all men will know you are my disciples, if you
love *one another.*
John 13:35

There is no greater witness to the unbelievers around us than showing them our love. We can do it in all kinds of ways—a smile, a word of encouragement, a random act of kindness. People notice when our attitudes and actions are self-serving, self-righteous, and not genuine. They can tell a fake when they see it. And if they can't, God can.

As Jesus' followers, we are to check our motives before going about our day. Our goal should always be to represent Him well, and there is no better way to do that than to show off His love.

Whom can you show off His love to today?

PRAYER

Lord Jesus, help me show Your genuine love to the people that cross my path today.

February 12

❧

LOVE = OBEDIENCE
---

*If you **love** me,*
you will obey what I command.
John 14:15

We can't have it both ways. We can't say we believe in Jesus Christ and love Jesus Christ and then live like we don't. In fact, this drives people away from Him faster than anything else. We are labeled as hypocrites, and our credibility is lost.

The Ten Commandments are timeless and foundational to our faith. Jesus came and died for our sins because we could never keep them perfectly, but they remain His standard and our plumb line to obey, for our good. When my grandson took a candy bar from a store, his sister discovered it and promptly told him, "There are only Ten Commandments. You need to know them and obey them!" How right she was! Love = obedience.

How well do you know the Ten Commandments, and how diligent are you to obey them?

PRAYER

Lord Jesus, help me prove my love for You by knowing and obeying Your commandments.

MOVE OVER

*If anyone **loves** me, he will obey
my teaching. My Father will **love** him
and we will come to him and make
our home with him.*
John 14:23

Can you think of anything better than the God who created the universe, and His Son whom He sent to die for us, living in us? This is Jesus' promise when we return His love with our love. When we do, we become His earthly temple and from that point forward, we face life with His Spirit living in us—loving us, guiding us, teaching us, comforting us, and holding us accountable to His Word. We will never be happy when we aren't. We have to move over and allow Him to move in. Then it becomes natural to want to please Him just like a child who knows they are loved wants to please their parents. Move over.

How attentive are you to the Holy Spirit's leading in your life?

PRAYER

Lord Jesus, help me be attentive and obedient to the Holy Spirit's leading in my life.

February 14

THE FIRST VALENTINE

*Greater **love** has no one than this,*
that he lay down his life for his friends.
John 15:13

Valentine's Day! We could say God started it. After all, it was His love that sent Jesus down to us and Jesus' love that sent Him to the cross. His love turned the world upside down. His teachings were completely counter cultural. His words, His lifestyle, and His example totally mesmerized the enormous crowds that followed Him. People had never seen anyone or heard anyone like Him before. He literally started a revolution. As His followers, we don't have to necessarily die to demonstrate our love for someone, but we do have to die to our own desires. We have to give up the rights to our own life and let Him use us as He sees fit. That, too, is dying.

Is your love for Jesus strong enough to let Him use you as He sees fit, regardless of the troubles that come your way?

PRAYER

Lord Jesus, that is a tough question and I can only pray that You help me love You regardless of the troubles that come my way.

POURED OUT

*Hope does not disappoint us,
because God has poured out his **love** into our hearts
by the Holy Spirit,
whom he has given us.*
Romans 5:5

K nowing God loves us is the basis for any hope we can have in this world. We can hope for all kinds of things—better grades, a more satisfying career, a happy marriage, good kids, a healthy life, a timely retirement, a painless death. Unfortunately, those hopes can fade and not turn out the way we wanted them to. But when we know and experience God's love deep in our heart, hope stays alive, and we can trust our ever-changing circumstances to the never-changing God who controls them. His love for us is greater than any obstacle, hardship, or uncertainty we will ever face, and His Holy Spirit is our constant companion to remind us.

What disappointment will you give to God today so He can revive your hope?

PRAYER

Lord Jesus, thank You for reviving my hope because You have poured out Your love to me. Now help me pour out my love to others on Your behalf.

February 16

KEEP PAYING

Let no debt remain outstanding, except the
*continuing debt to **love** one another.*
Romans 13:8

J esus keeps coming back to this command to love others, because it is so foundational to our love for Him. If we truly love Him, we can't help but love others, because He created them just as He created us. Who are we to choose whom we are to love when He loves everyone?

This was so important to Jesus that the second most important commandment—second to loving Him—is to love our neighbors as ourselves (Matthew 22:38). That's a tall order, and it doesn't stop there because it never ends. We owe Him a debt to love, because His love paid the debt for our sin. Out of sheer gratitude, it is the one debt we should continue to pay until we meet Him face to face. Keep paying.

Whom can you love for Jesus because He loves you?

PRAYER

Lord Jesus, show me whom I can love today because You love me.

GENUINE LOVE

Love *is patient, love is kind. It does not envy, it does not boast, it is not proud.*
1 Corinthians 13:4

We hear these words read at weddings with the hope of getting the marriage off to a good start. Hopefully, they will. But it's important to realize that Paul's description of love adds a whole new dimension to ours. We can think of love as a temporary or conditional emotion—one that we can control according to our whims, and our circumstances, and what it's going to do for us. But if God's love is truly in us, we will take these words to heart and love beyond our own strength and insecurities. We will put ourselves and our own needs aside and strive to love the way Jesus loves us. His love is patient and kind. It does not envy or boast. It is not prideful. It is genuine.

What will you change in the way you love so it is more genuine?

PRAYER

Lord Jesus, help me make the necessary changes so my love for people is more like Yours.

February 18

COUNT ON IT

Love *never fails.*
1 Corinthians 13:8

Think of all the things that come and go in your life. We can plan out our future and even what we will do tomorrow, only to have our plans change and our hopes for the future fail to come true. Life can take a totally different path than the one we thought we were on. Plans change, circumstances change, people and relationships change, places change, ambitions and desires change, opportunities change, health changes. But in any situation or set of circumstances we find ourselves in, if we know we are loved, we will survive. Love never fails because God is love and He never fails. We can count on His love for us, and we can count on Him to love through us.

What situation are you in today that you need to count on God's love to get you through?

PRAYER

Lord Jesus, help me count on Your love today.

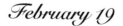

February 19

LOVE WINS

*And now these three remain: faith, hope and **love**. But the greatest of these is **love**.*
1 Corinthians 13:13

Love trumps all things, even faith and hope, because without love, what is our faith in and what are we hoping for? Faith and hope are needed to help us live with confidence in this life and look forward to the next. But once we have passed from here to THERE, neither will be necessary, because we will be living in the reality of both. Our years of believing and trusting Jesus will be over when we see Him face to face, and our years of hoping will be over because our hopes will be fulfilled. But love will remain, because we will be in the presence of LOVE itself for all eternity.

How is your idea of love changing as we study it from God's point of view?

PRAYER

Lord Jesus, help my love become more and more like Yours.

GIVE CHEERFULLY

*Each man should give what he has decided in his
heart to give, not reluctantly or under compulsion,
for God **loves** a cheerful giver.*
2 Corinthians 9:7

As a mother, grandmother, and great-grandmother, I love to buy gifts for my family. I think about what I want to give them way ahead of time. I bait them to drop little hints, so I get them what they want. I do my research to find the perfect thing and set aside the money I want to spend. Then I make the big purchase and wrap it all up. I can't wait to give it to them. It is so much fun to give gifts to the people we love. Likewise, we should plan ahead exactly what we want to give God instead of fumbling for our wallet in church and pulling out the first bill we see. God loves a cheerful giver not a have-to giver. Give cheerfully.

Are you a cheerful giver or a have-to giver?

PRAYER

Lord Jesus, help me show my love for You in the way I give to You.

February 21

HAVE IT ALL

*But the fruit of the Spirit is **love**, joy, peace, patience, kindness, goodness, faithfulness, gentleness and self-control.*
Galatians 5:22-23

Love is the first benefit of God's Spirit living in us. Without experiencing His love, we cannot give out His love; we cannot experience true joy or peace; we cannot endure hardship or suffering in His strength; we cannot express kindness in His Name; we cannot be good in His sight; we cannot be faithful to Him; we cannot be gentle like He is; and we cannot maintain self-control in difficult situations. Imagine what the world would be like if everyone had the Holy Spirit of God living in them! Imagine the difference in nations, cities, towns, churches, universities, schools, and families! We can't change the world, but we can change the environment we live in by maximizing His Sprit's power within us. We can have it all and use it for His glory!

How much fruit of Jesus' Spirit do you want?

PRAYER

Lord Jesus, help me want all the fruit of Your Spirit and use it for Your glory.

February 22

CHECK YOUR MOTIVES

*The goal of this command is **love**,
which comes from a pure heart and a
good conscience and a sincere faith.*
1 Timothy 1:5

God is omniscient, meaning He knows all things. We can't hide anything from Him, not even the motives of our heart. His love for us has one motive, to save us from eternal damnation. Jesus came with the pure motive to fulfill His Father's plan of salvation for us, which He did on the cross. As believers we are to check our motives and make sure they are not self-serving or aligned with any other purpose than to honor and please Him. His Holy Spirit in us holds us accountable and gives us a clear conscience when our motives are pure, and our faith is sincere. Check your motives.

Is your motive to love others pure and sincere or selfish and self-serving?

PRAYER

Lord Jesus, help my love for others to be pure and sincere and show me when it is not.

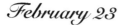

February 23

🦢

BEWARE!

---

*For the **love** of money is the root of all kinds of evil.*
Some people, eager for money, have wandered from
the faith and pierced themselves with many griefs.
1 Timothy 6:10

L ots of things in this world compete for our love, but probably nothing more so than money. After all, we are led to believe that money can buy us anything—even love itself. But as soon as we stray down this path, we are in trouble. Soon we find that greediness takes over, because we never have enough. As a result, sorrow instead of satisfaction awaits us. Money is necessary and money has its place, but beware! It can never buy faith.

What place does money have in your life?

PRAYER

Lord Jesus, please give me a healthy attitude toward money. Help me to see it as Your provision and use it wisely.

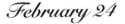

TRUE LOVE

*Above all, **love** each other deeply,*
*because **love** covers a multitude of sins.*
1 Peter 4:8

True love comes from the very core of us. It is honest, sincere, genuine, intentional, robust, fervent. It is loving to the max. It is love on steroids. It goes beyond our natural ability to love. It is born in us when we become born again. It is a picture of God's love for us when He died on the cross for our sins. Therefore, it is powerful enough to help us forgive others who have wronged us and strong enough to keep us from holding a grudge against them, or making them feel like we do. True love covers a multitude of sins.

Whom do you need to love with this kind of love so you can forgive them and move on?

PRAYER

Lord Jesus, I can only love like You, because of You. Help me pass on Your love to others.

ALL IN THE FAMILY

*Dear friends, since God so **loved** us,*
*we also ought to **love** one another.*
1 John 4:11

God expressed His ultimate love for us by sending His Son to die for us, so we could be reconciled to Him and spend eternity with Him. He could not have done anything greater than what He has done. The cross stands in the middle of human history and beckons us to it, because it is the physical, visible, historical, documented proof of His love. When we accept His love and His sacrifice on our behalf, we are signing on to His prescribed teachings. And we are joining His elite circle of 'friends.' Therefore, it is our privilege to love and care for each other, because His love brought us together in the first place. We are family.

What can you do for another believer today?

PRAYER

Lord Jesus, show me whom I can reach out to in the family today.

February 26

LIVE WITHOUT FEAR

*But perfect **love** drives out fear, because fear has to do with punishment. The one who fears is not made perfect in **love**.*
1 John 4:18

Believers have a reverential fear of God, but we do not fear His judgment for our sin, because Jesus paid the price for it on the cross. Without claiming His sacrifice on our behalf, we should fear His judgment, because sin demands it. God would not be the just and holy God He is without His judgment. It only follows then, that perfect love is when His love lives in us. When we embrace His love, we live without fear, because we know we are safe in Him, free of His judgment, and free of the punishment our sin deserves. Live without fear and pass His offer of freedom on to others.

Are you living without fear because Jesus has saved you from judgment?

PRAYER

Lord Jesus, thank You for my salvation in You so I do not have to fear Your judgment. Help me share this great news with others.

PUT DOWN THE BURDEN

*This is **love** for God: to obey his commands.
And his commands are not burdensome.*
1 John 5:3

Burdensome sounds heavy, hard, and depressing. Unfortunately, the secular world views God's commandments as burdensome, and therefore people apart from God don't want any part of Him or feel any obligation to obey His commandments. But actually the opposite is true. In fact, that's exactly why He gave them to us.

Living in disobedience to God is burdensome, because we are carrying the burden of our sin. When we are living in obedience to Him, we are free of the burden, because Jesus carried it to the cross and left it there. Therefore, His commands are not burdensome. They free us from the burden, and we are happier and healthier as a result. Put down the burden.

Are you living under the burden of disobedience or in the freedom of obedience? Time to put the burden down.

PRAYER

Lord Jesus, help me love Your commandments and want to obey them because they are for my good.

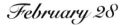

NOTHING BUT THE BLOOD

*To him who **loves** us and has freed us
from our sins by his blood.*
Revelation 1:5

The secular world does not like to hear about the blood of Jesus. People mock it, scoff it, ignore it, and reject it. But it does not change the fact that only the blood of Jesus Christ saves us from sin and frees us to live the life we were created to live. God established animal sacrifices early in the Old Testament as His prescribed way to receive forgiveness. Life is in the blood, and a life had to be taken to pay the price for sin.

Animal sacrifices pointed to Jesus' death on the cross and therefore, became obsolete. His death was a once-for-all sacrifice for the sins of the world. Nothing but His blood would pay the price for our sin. Hallelujah! What a Savior!

Do you see the blood of Jesus as precious or repulsive?

PRAYER

Lord Jesus, thank You for shedding Your blood on my behalf. Help my life reflect my gratitude.

FIRST LOVE

Yet I hold this against you:
*You have forsaken your first **love**.*
Revelation 2:4

Believers in Ephesus had started out strong in their faith. They had worked hard to build their church; they had persevered and endured hardships. And they had kept false teaching from infiltrating or watering down the truth of the gospel. In other words, they were an exemplary church, and yet, they had forgotten their first love. Their work for Jesus had overshadowed their love for Jesus. It can happen so easily.

We can begin to worship our work for our Savior instead of worshiping HIM. Let's wake up every day and remember He wants to be our first love.

Are you allowing your work for Jesus to overshadow your worship of Him?

PRAYER

Lord Jesus, You deserve to be my first love. Help me always keep You there.

March

FEAR

❧

How do we keep **fear**
from sidelining us on our journey of faith?

YOU ARE NOT ALONE

*Be strong and courageous. Do not be **afraid** or terrified . . . for the Lord your God goes with you; he will never leave you nor forsake you.*
Deuteronomy 31:6

The year 2020 will long be remembered as the year COVID-19 became a global pandemic. It was declared a national emergency by the president in March. Fear gripped this nation and the world as lockdowns were enforced and the economy tanked. As we continue our journey of faith, it's only fitting that we focus on fear this month because we never know when the next crisis will hit.

I am in my second year of being a widow, and nothing has lessened my fear and given me greater comfort in a very scary world than knowing God is with me in whatever lies ahead. I am not alone, and neither are you.

What has you gripped in fear right now? Will you give it to Jesus and trust He is with you and will never leave you?

PRAYER

Lord Jesus, help me turn to You with my fears and know You are always with me.

March 2

CHOOSE CAREFULLY

*For great is the Lord and most worthy of praise; he is
to be **feared** above all gods.*
1 Chronicles 16:25

No other god is worthy of our praise or worship, because no other god has the power to create or is sovereign over people and nations. No other god is living. Most importantly, no other god came to this earth and died for our sins, and then rose from the dead to prove we will be resurrected too.

Every god of every other religion died and is still dead. Dead gods cannot see what we are going through, hear our prayers, or do anything to help us—let alone save us. And yet we worship these gods for the simple reason they have no power over us and therefore cannot hold us accountable. The choice is ours, but we better choose carefully.

Are you prepared to defend your faith in Jesus, as the living God, to people of other faiths?

PRAYER

Lord Jesus, thank You for being the only living God who I can talk to and trust to take care of me. Help me be prepared to share You with others.

GOOD FEAR

*The **fear** of the Lord is pure,*
enduring forever.
Psalm 19:9

Reverential fear of God is foundational to our Christian faith, because it is based on the first commandment. We are to love Him above everything else. We are to honor Him and order our life in alignment with His will, because nothing else will help us survive in a world that is dominated by evil. Reverential fear of God will strengthen us and sustain us even through the worst of times. When we put Him first, all His resources are at our disposal to call upon, and we will experience His presence and power like never before.

There are many things we can fear today that can harm us. But a healthy fear of God is pure, and we will carry it with us to Heaven. That's a good fear!

What is your fear of God based on?

PRAYER

Lord Jesus, I fear You because You are God and as such deserve and demand my first allegiance and obedience. Help me give it to You.

OUR SHEPHERD

Even though I walk through
the valley of the shadow of death,
*I will **fear** no evil, for you are with me;*
your rod and your staff comfort me.
Psalm 23:4

During my husband's last year of life, we worked on memorizing the twenty-third psalm which includes this verse. Nothing brought him more comfort during those difficult days, and nothing has given me more comfort since.

Knowing God is with us during the valleys of life when we are most vulnerable and most afraid of what lies ahead gives us the strength and the fortitude to lean on Him and keep on walking. His rod and staff symbolize His authority and protection over our lives and help us visualize His care for us like a shepherd over his flock. The shepherd protected his flock from danger. Jesus does the same for us. Let Him guide you. He will!

How are you allowing Jesus to guide you, and what comfort is it giving you?

PRAYER

Lord Jesus, I know You care for us like a shepherd cares for his sheep. Help me lean on You for Your guidance and comfort.

WHAT ARE WE AFRAID OF?

The Lord is my light and my salvation—
*whom shall I **fear**? The Lord is the stronghold*
*of my life—of whom shall I be **afraid**?*
Psalm 27:1

There's a lot to be afraid of today. Political upheaval, social unrest, deadly viruses, violent protests, uncontrolled lawlessness, and a growing disdain for the things of God. In fact, Christians are being silenced by the voices that seek to destroy our country and destroy our faith.

There is only one light in this darkness and that is the light of Jesus Christ. He is the only answer to the sin that is sweeping our nation and our only hope for salvation. With Him on our side, we can overcome the evil. Without Him on our side, the evil will overcome us. It's time to decide, are we too afraid to stand up against it? Or are we too afraid not to?

What are you most afraid of today and how will you depend on Jesus to help you through it?

PRAYER

Lord Jesus, help me take my fears to You and depend on You to help me.

March 6

BE DELIVERED

I sought the Lord, and he answered me;
*he delivered me from all my **fears**.*
Psalm 34:4

When I was asked to teach a weekly Bible study to 500 women, my immediate reaction was abject fear. I was a college drop-out and had no teaching experience. The only thing I brought to the table was I loved Jesus and I loved His Word.

So I opened my Bible and asked Him to help me, because I was terrified to say YES, but even more terrified to say no. This verse, Psalm 34:4 stared me in the face. I wrote it in the folder for my notes and read it every week for the next eighteen years. What is God asking you to do today that you are afraid to do? Don't let fear stop you. Be delivered and be blessed.

Are you willing to take a risk and do something you don't think you can do but God does?

PRAYER

Lord Jesus, help me be willing to take a risk for You and trust You to deliver me from the fear of doing it.

March 7

TRUST JESUS

Fear the Lord, you his saints,
*for those who **fear** him lack nothing.*
Psalm 34:9

D o you ever feel like you don't have the courage to stand against the evil we see in our world today? Do you ever feel like your opinion or your effort doesn't count anyway? Do you stand down instead of standing up? This is a wake-up call to all believers!

When we fear God above everything else, there is nothing we lack to stand up against the evil that threatens to destroy us. We have all the power of Almighty God on our side and nothing will prevail against it. But He needs our unswerving trust and commitment. Then He meets us where we are and supplies what we need. EVERYTHING we need! Let's trust Him to give it to us.

What do you need God to do for you to help you stand up for Him today?

PRAYER

Lord Jesus, thank You for giving me what I need to stand up for You.

March 8

PAY ATTENTION

An oracle is within my heart concerning the sinfulness
*of the wicked: there is no **fear** of God before his eyes.*
Psalm 36:1

Breaking News keeps us abreast of the increasing evil in our world. We can't help but wonder where it's all coming from, and why it's getting so much worse. The writer of this psalm must have had the same problem in his day and wondered the same thing. God gave him the answer in the form of a divine announcement or revelation, an oracle. The reason is simple, there is no fear of God in their eyes.

In other words, people who don't believe and have no interest in God don't think they are accountable to Him. But we are accountable to God, whether we believe in Him or not. We all need to pay attention to that!

How does your reverential fear of God keep you account-able to Him?

PRAYER

Lord Jesus, help me be accountable to You, because You know what is best for me, and it proves I belong to You.

DON'T MISS IT

*You alone are to be **feared**. Who can stand before*
you when you are angry?
Psalm 76:7

W e like to hear about God's love, not His anger. But His anger or wrath is justified because of sin. He has to be angry at sin because of what it has done to His creation. Sin separates us from Him and denies us our rightful place with Him.

But Jesus came and stood in the gap for us. He took our sins upon Himself and took the punishment we deserve. Because of Jesus, instead of experiencing God's wrath, we will experience the full measure of His love in His presence forever! Our greatest fear should be missing out on that! Don't miss it.

Have you experienced God's forgiveness, so you won't face His anger for your sin?

PRAYER

Lord Jesus, thank You for forgiving me.

GET WISDOM

*The **fear** of the Lord is the beginning of wisdom; all who follow his precepts have good understanding.*
Psalm 111:10

We need wisdom in this crazy world—wisdom to discern the truth, wisdom to make the right choices, wisdom to raise our kids and grandkids with God's values instead of the changing values of this world.

Only God can give us such wisdom because He is the source of wisdom. It's up to each of us to go back to His Word and to His commandments, because only there do we find the framework to live His way instead of our way. This is the Information Age because of the massive information available to us via the Internet. But true wisdom only comes from God. It's time we go to Him to get it.

How deliberate are you in seeking God's wisdom so you can live according to His standard instead of the standards of this world?

PRAYER

Lord Jesus, help me seek Your wisdom each day so I live according to Your Word.

GET A GOOD NIGHT'S SLEEP

*But whoever listens to me will live in safety
and be at ease, without **fear** of harm.*
Proverbs 1:33

One of the advantages of living in the age of the Internet is the apps we can access that give us help on almost anything we need. A popular app today recites Bible verses in a calm soothing voice to help us sleep.

Even though every generation has probably felt the same, we need our sleep more than ever, because there's never been more to be afraid of. Our safety and security have never been more threatened, and we yearn for a peaceful existence. The inventor of that app knew what King Solomon knew millennia ago—that God is our only source of safety and only in Him can we be at ease in a stressful world. Read your Bible and get a good night's sleep.

What do you do when you can't sleep?

PRAYER

Lord Jesus, help me find release from my anxiety and stress in Your Word, to calm my spirit and relieve my fears.

March 12

THE RED LINE

*A wise man **fears** God and shuns evil,*
but a fool is hotheaded and reckless.
Proverbs 14:16

We're living in a time of great division within our country that goes beyond the political or racial division we see on our screens. The division that will destroy us as a nation is spiritual. It's the division that began with Adam and Eve in the garden. They chose to be "hotheaded and reckless" and turned away from God. Their act of disobedience became the Biblical definition of fool.

God describes a fool as a person that rejects Him (Psalm 14:1). He established the first "red line." He is on one side, and we are wise when we stand with Him. Satan is on the other side luring us to cross the line like Adam and Eve did, and we are a fool if we do. Don't cross that red line.

How do your attitudes and actions reflect that you stand with God?

PRAYER

Lord Jesus, help me shun evil and live in obedience to You.

THE RIGHT SECURITY

*He who **fears** the Lord has a secure fortress,*
and for his children it will be a refuge.
Proverbs 14:26

G ated communities are popular today. We like the security of a coded entry and watching the gate close behind us. It makes us feel like we are safe inside the gate, and no harm will come to us or our family. Yet we know how false that sense of security can be because people bent on evil can break down gates and destroy lives in a nanosecond.

True security is only found in God and His promises, because His security is eternal, so no matter what happens to us here on earth, we are safe with Him forever. He is our secure fortress in an insecure world. His is the right security!

Are you living behind the false security the world offers or behind the eternal security God offers? How are you teaching your family to find their security in Him?

PRAYER

Lord Jesus, please help me set the example in my family of trusting You for my security.

BE SAFE

---

*Fear of man will prove to be a snare,
but whoever trusts in the Lord is kept safe.*
Proverbs 29:25

This country is currently experiencing blatant lawlessness like we have never seen before. Less than a mile from my house, vandals recently smashed store windows and broke in to steal whatever they could grab and carry out with them. I watched in horror as the mob moved closer to my neighborhood. Family and friends texted. We prayed. The mob left. The violence was quelled.

And once again, our verse for today was proven true—what can man do to me when God is taking care of me? Whether we live or die, we are safe when we belong to Jesus, because He controls it all. Be safe in Jesus.

Whom or what are you fearful of today? Will you give it to Jesus and experience His security?

PRAYER

Lord Jesus, help me give my fears to You and find the security I seek.

DO YOUR DUTY

*Fear God and keep his commandments,
for this is the whole duty of man.*
Ecclesiastes 12:13

God's commandments are His standard for people to live by. Yet today they can't be posted in our government buildings or taught in our schools. And we see the result. Children are growing up with no boundaries of right and wrong, no respect for authority, no knowledge of God, and therefore, no fear or reverence for Him. We have to ask ourselves, what kind of world will they grow up to?

God did not give us His commandments as a suggestion. They are our duty to obey so our lives will go well. It's time for a spiritual checkup to make sure we know them and obey them, and then do our part to make sure they are being taught. It's our duty.

What can you do to make sure the Ten Commandments are known and followed in your family?

PRAYER

Lord Jesus, help me do my duty to You and to my family by making sure the Ten Commandments are posted and followed.

HE WILL COME

*Say to those with **fearful** hearts,*
*"Be strong, do not **fear**; your God will come."*
Isaiah 35:4

There is nothing worse than a fearful heart. It leads to headaches, high blood pressure, and other stress-related issues. Fear is not healthy.

The antidote for fear is trust. And not just trust in ourselves to work through a problem or trust in someone else to help us through it, but trust in God. Only God can give us the strength, focus and assurance that He is in control of whatever we are fearful of. And only God is always available to help us. I love keeping a journal and over the years, I have recorded the times I was most fearful. Without fail, Jesus has always met me in those fears. If you are fearful right now, call out to Him and He will come!

What do you do when fear grips you?

PRAYER

Lord Jesus, You are my God, help me reach out to You with my fears instead of relying on myself or others.

REMEMBER WHOSE YOU ARE

*Do not **fear**, for I am with you;*
do not be dismayed, for I am your God.
Isaiah 41:10

We can be strong in a scary world because God is with us. He is stronger than any enemy we face or fear we have. When I am afraid, it helps me to think about who God is and why I can trust Him. I think though His attributes in alphabetical order. He is Almighty, He is the Beginning and the end, He is the Creator, the Deliverer, etc. And soon my fears begin to melt into the reality that He who is with me is far greater than anyone or anything that is against me (1 John 4:4).

Remembering who we belong to gives us comfort and strength in times of fear and stress. How can we be dismayed when God is with us? This is a good day to remember Whose you are.

Will you give some time to thinking through God's attributes so He can strengthen you the next time you feel dismayed?

PRAYER

Lord Jesus, help me remember who You are when I am dismayed so I don't succumb to fear.

March 18

SUMMONED BY NAME

Fear *not for I have redeemed you;*
I have summoned you by name; you are mine.
Isaiah 43:1

It boggles our minds to think that the God of the universe calls us by name and tells us we are His. But He does! I will never forget the first time I read this verse and cried as I did because I had just received devastating news. Nothing could have stopped my tears or comforted me more than knowing God loved me this much! It became the pivotal point in my faith. I began to look at everything from that perspective instead of the perspective of fear, doubt, and insecurity.

It's a life-changer when we know we are not just a number with God but a person He loves so deeply that He knows our name, calls us by name, and reminds us we are His.

Does knowing Jesus calls you by name relieve your fear and renew your strength for what you're going through today?

PRAYER

Lord Jesus, thank You for knowing me this intimately. Help me draw strength from that today.

BE TOUGH

*Do not **fear** the reproach of men*
or be terrified by their insults.
Isaiah 51:7

S ticks and stones will break my bones, but names will never hurt me. Did you ever hear that growing up? It was our go-to on the playground when other kids tried to bully us, and it usually worked to drive them away.

The words may be different than Isaiah wrote centuries ago, but the message is the same. The only time we should fear someone else's disapproval is when we know they are speaking for God and He confirms it in His Word. And we should never be terrified by another's insults, because that is against His Word. Jesus sets the example of toughness for us. He did not fear His enemies' disapproval and He walked away from their insults. Be tough.

How do you react to criticism? Do you pray and align it with God's Word, so you know whether or not it's from Him?

PRAYER

Lord Jesus, help me know when criticism is justified, and help me walk away from insults because they are never justified.

JESUS IS KING

---

*Who should not **fear** you,*
O King of the nations? This is your due.
Jeremiah 10:7

A s I write this, the nations are in turmoil because they do not fear God as the King of all nations. We can't help but wonder how long He is going to put up with such arrogance, insubordination, and stupidity.

But we do know there is a limit to His patience, and we do know that Jesus is coming again to establish His kingdom on earth. He will rule the world the way God intended it to be ruled in the first place. Until then we can expect continued upheaval, unrest, wars, and rumors of wars, because God is letting us have our way. But our way will end, and His way will prevail. He may have come the first time as a baby, but He's coming again as King.

Do you pray for our nation and government authorities to bow to Jesus as King of this nation and all nations?

PRAYER

Lord Jesus, help me remember that You are King of all nations and to pray for my country to honor You as such.

RESERVATION CONFIRMED

A scroll of remembrance was written
*in his presence concerning those who **feared***
the Lord and honored his name.
Malachi 3:16

D id you know that Jesus keeps a personal address book? He records all the names of people who have been to the cross and accepted His sacrifice for sin on their behalf. If our name is in it, our reservation is made and confirmed in Heaven. If it is not, we will be turned away.

We like to think that God is not that strict or that definite, and that since He is such a loving God, He won't turn anyone away. But that is man's thinking not His thinking. His Word makes it clear that we are not lost in the masses. He knows everything about us and can't wait to spend eternity with us. That's why He records our name. Make sure your reservation is confirmed.

Are you sure your name is recorded in Jesus' scroll of remembrance?

PRAYER

Lord Jesus, thank You for confirming my reservation with You and help me lead others to make theirs.

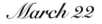

BE SAFE, DEAD OR ALIVE

*Do not be **afraid** of those who kill the body but
cannot kill the soul. Rather, be **afraid** of the One who
can destroy both soul and body in hell.*
Matthew 10:28

Fear is at an all-time high today because of the escalation of violence in our cities. No place seems to be exempt. Innocent people are randomly shot. Drive by shootings are an everyday occurrence. The aftermath is horrific. Children can't play in their yards, and parents are carrying guns because law enforcement is compromised. What's the solution?

Jesus is the solution. He confirmed it with the promise that we have nothing to fear when we belong to Him, because we are safe, dead or alive. But if we do not belong to Him, we have every reason to be afraid, because He has the power to send us to Hell. Jesus is our only safety in a scary world.

Whom can you share Jesus with today, so they are safe in Him too?

PRAYER

Lord Jesus, thank You that no matter what happens to my body, my soul is safe with You. Help me share this hope with others.

IT'S ALL YOURS

*Do not be **afraid**, little flock,
for your Father has been pleased
to give you the kingdom.*
Luke 12:32

Jesus spoke these words to His frightened disciples, as well as the people following Him who were looking for safety in the scary world they lived in. We are looking for the same safety today. He wants us to change our focus from seeking safety in the materialism of this world to seeking safety in the spiritual benefits of His Kingdom.

The world is Satan's kingdom and offers temporary pleasure and false security. God's kingdom offers permanent pleasure and eternal security. Satan creates fear; God guarantees peace. Jesus told believers then and He tells us now, don't settle for anything less than God's Kingdom. It's all yours. Take it.

Are you settling for anything less than all the Father wants to give you?

PRAYER

Lord Jesus, help me say no to Satan's kingdom, which may be alluring for the moment but very temporary, and yes to God's kingdom whose benefits are out of this world.

KEEP THE FEAR
AND GROW THE CHURCH

Then the church . . . grew in numbers,
*living in the **fear** of the Lord.*
Acts 9:31

The Church grows when unbelievers want what believers have. The opposite is also true. Unbelievers don't want any part of the Church when they see hypocrisy and division. Why would they, when there's enough of that in the world.

The early Church turned the world upside down, because they had learned from Jesus and were living like Jesus. It caused a spiritual revolution that remains with us today. But the Church needs help. We need to be less politically correct and more biblically sound. We need to hear less about social issues and focus on the gospel. We need to stop fearing the world and start fearing God. Keep the fear and grow the Church.

How are you helping your church grow? Are you hindering its growth in any way?

PRAYER

Lord Jesus, help me be a constructive member of my church so others will want to join.

THE PERFECT FATHER

[God] accepts men from every nation
*who **fear** him and do what is right.*
Acts 10:35

God is the perfect Father. He does not have favorites. His love reaches out to every person of every nationality, race, color, and creed. From every nation on every continent on earth. From every economic and educational background. The ground is level at the foot of the cross, and He beckons all people to meet Him there.

America is the most blessed nation on earth, because our founding fathers feared God and chose to align with Him. But we are in danger of losing His blessing, because we fear losing control more than we fear Him. It's time to stand up and speak up for the freedoms this country is founded on. It's time to let God be God. He is the perfect Father.

What can you do in your sphere of influence to stand up and speak up for the values this nation was founded on?

PRAYER

Lord Jesus, help me be a voice for You so our nation continues to receive Your blessing.

DON'T MISPLACE YOUR FEAR

*Since, then, we know what it is to **fear** the Lord,*
we try to persuade men.
2 Corinthians 5:11

Are we as excited to share God's love, grace, mercy, and forgiveness in Jesus Christ as we are a great vacation spot, fabulous restaurant, or the latest movie? Are we as eager to recommend Jesus as we are a good landscaper, painter, or hairdresser? Are we as prepared to share why we believe in Him as we are our opinions on a myriad of different subjects?

Paul says that since we know what it means to love Jesus, we should be just as excited, eager, and prepared to share Him as we are all the other wonderful things we experience. And yet too often, our fear of the Lord is replaced with fear of rejection. Don't misplace your fear! Share the Lord.

How eager and prepared are you to share your faith when the opportunity comes up?

PRAYER

Lord Jesus, there is nothing more important than telling the world about You. Help me be eager and prepared to do it.

WORK FOR GOD

Therefore, my dear friends . . .
continue to work out your
*salvation with **fear** and trembling.*
Philippians 2:12

This verse can be confusing because some people think it means we have to work for our salvation or at least continue to work for it until we die. But nothing could be further from the truth.

The Bible makes it clear that salvation is a one-time gift we receive when we come to Christ for forgiveness of our sins and accept His sacrifice on our behalf. At that moment, we are born again, and nothing will ever take that new life away from us. But that new life is the very thing that motivates us to live for Him going forward, because we love Him too much not to. Enjoy your new life and work for God.

Do you work for God because you think you have to or because you love Him too much not to?

PRAYER

Lord Jesus, help my love for You motivate everything I do.

FAITH OVER FEAR

*For God has not given us a spirit
of **fear**, but of power and of love
and of a sound mind.*
2 Timothy 1:7 (NKJV)

Fear is a great friend when there is something to be fearful of, like a fire, and a great enemy when there is nothing to fear. God has given us the emotion of fear, first, to bring us to Him because we fear His judgment on our sin, and second, as a warning device or alarm system to warn us of impending disaster. He never intended for us to live in a state of perpetual anxiety like so many people do today.

On the contrary, God gives us power and a sound mind through the reading of His Word to be able to overcome our fears and live in faith instead. Faith in God and His Word will always overcome our fears. Choose faith over fear.

How much time do you spend in His Word so your fears are overcome with faith?

PRAYER

Lord Jesus, help me turn to You for the strength I need to live by faith instead of fear.

BE RESPONSIBLE

*Show proper respect to everyone: Love the
brotherhood of believers, **fear** God, honor the king.*
1 Peter 2:17

Every human being is created by God and bears His image. This separates us from the animal kingdom. He has given us the emotions, heart, mind, and soul capable of relating to Him and to each other the way He relates to us. He calls us into a personal relationship with Him so He can build His kingdom on this earth and enjoy our company in Heaven.

But along with this gift comes responsibility. We are responsible for our relationship with Him, our relationship with other believers, and our relationship with everyone else. The world would be a better place if we took our responsibility seriously. Let's put God first, love our fellow believers, and respect others.

How does your fear of God motivate you to love your fellow believers and respect everyone else?

PRAYER

Lord Jesus, help me love my fellow believers. And help me respect those who don't believe so perhaps they will.

March 30

EMBRACE HIS LOVE

*There is no **fear** in love.*
But perfect love drives out fear,
*because **fear** has to do with punishment.*
1 John 4:18

There is nothing worse than doing something you know is wrong and then waiting to be punished for it. Back in the fifties, parents didn't hesitate to spank their kids when they disobeyed. Mine were no different. I remember sneaking out of the house with my brother and our parents driving around the neighborhood until they found us. We both knew what was coming and were not disappointed. But it cured us. I don't remember ever sneaking out again.

Thank God for Jesus. There is no fear of punishment when we belong to Him, because He took our punishment for us and now we are free to embrace His love.

Have you fully embraced God's love because you know Jesus has taken the punishment you deserve for your sin?

PRAYER

Lord Jesus, thank You for taking the punishment I deserve for my sin so I am free to embrace Your love.

GIVE GOD THE GLORY

***Fear** God and give him glory, because the hour of his judgment has come. Worship him who made the heavens, the earth, the sea and the springs of water.*
Revelation 14:7

I t's easy to succumb to the fears of our time. But we can choose to live in faith instead, because God is in control. This is His world. He made it. He sustains it. He has a plan for it. He died and rose again for it. And He is coming again to make things right.

In the meantime, we are to focus on Him, worship Him, and give Him the credit He deserves, because He is greater than any evil we experience. It is our privilege and responsibility to make Him known. At the end of the day, everything we are afraid of will be gone, and the only thing that will matter is what we did with Him. Give up your fears and give Him the glory!

What fears will you give up, and choose to focus on God instead?

PRAYER

Lord Jesus, You deserve my attention more than my fears. Help me let go of them and focus on You.

April

TRUTH

❧

Knowing the **truth** is
essential on our journey of faith.

WHAT GOD DESIRES

*Surely you desire **truth**
in the inner parts; you teach me
wisdom in the inmost place.*
Psalm 51:6

As we continue our journey of faith, the most important thing to God is that we know the truth and our lives reflect it. Contrary to what the world thinks, truth is not murky, ambiguous, or unattainable, because God makes it very clear. There is only one truth, and it's Him. He is the absolute for every generation to know, and His Word makes Him knowable.

We know God in the Old Testament through four great events—Creation, the Fall, the Flood, and Babel—and four great men: Abraham, Isaac, Jacob, and Joseph. In the New Testament, we know Him through the Person of His Son, Jesus Christ. God wants us to know Him, so we know the truth and live by it.

Are you seeking the truth? It is only found in Jesus Christ.

PRAYER

Lord Jesus, in this confusing world, help me to know You as the truth I am looking for.

❧

MAKE THE TRADE

*Your righteousness is
everlasting and your law is **true**.*
Psalm 119:142

Righteousness is right behavior. God has always acted righteously toward His people. Jesus Christ is the personification of righteousness. We can't be righteous without Him, because no matter how hard we try, there is always something wrong with our righteousness. Apart from Jesus, our motives, attitudes, and actions are self-centered and self-serving.

We need the righteousness of Jesus Christ, and it becomes ours when we come to the cross for forgiveness. We give Him our sins—our unrighteousness—and He gives us His righteousness. As a result, we are given everlasting life. We have His Word. Make the trade!

Have you been to the cross to give Jesus your sins in exchange for His righteousness? It's a trade with everlasting value.

PRAYER

Lord Jesus, thank You that Your righteousness becomes mine at the cross. Help me receive it and live out Your righteousness in my life.

LISTEN TO HIM

*I, the Lord speak the **truth**;*
I declare what is right.
Isaiah 45:19

We are all looking for truth today. We are looking for truth in our government, our city councils, our schools and universities, our churches, and certainly in our homes. But truth has lost its way. Truth has become whatever we want it to be. Truth has gone from being an absolute or a constant that never changes, to being just a commodity we can pick up along the way from a myriad of different sources.

Many people don't know the truth and therefore, can't speak the truth. It's time to go back to the basics. It's time to see what God says about truth, because He is truth. He speaks it, He declares it, and we can trust it. Listen to Him.

What is truth to you?

PRAYER

Lord Jesus, help me turn to You for the truth. You speak it and You declare it. Help me hear it.

April 4

BE FOUND

*__Truth__ is nowhere to be found, and whoever shuns evil
becomes a prey.*
Isaiah 59:15

The Old Testament prophet Isaiah is confessing the sins of his nation, the nation of Israel. But he could be speaking of any nation today, including ours. When we reject truth, we are really rejecting God. Unfortunately, our nation is turning away from Him, and we are living with the consequences.

Moral decline, broken families, lack of respect for authority, increased crime and blatant lawlessness, among other sins, are taking us on a downward spiral. Speaking against this trend puts believers at risk. But speak up we must! We must stand firm on God's Word and be found to be people who know the truth, speak the truth, and live the truth.

How much time do you give to reading the Bible so you can know and defend the truth?

PRAYER

Lord Jesus, help me be found by You to be a person who lives by the truth.

WHEN JESUS RETURNS

*Then Jerusalem will be
called the City of **Truth.***
Zechariah 8:3

Believers look forward to the day when Jesus Christ returns to make things right. He will return to His city, Jerusalem, and rule the world the way He intended it to be ruled in the first place. The Old Testament prophet Zechariah wrote these words centuries before Jesus was even born when sin, instead of truth, prevailed just as it does today. And now, all these centuries later, we are more determined than ever to reject God's truth and make up our own.

But God will not be mocked. His patience will come to an end. Someday, Jesus will return and reclaim His city as the City of Truth, and His truth will prevail. What a day that will be!

Whom can you share this truth of Jesus' return with today?

PRAYER

Lord Jesus, show me whom I can share the truth of Your return with, so they can look forward to it too.

April 6

REPRESENT GOD WELL

*Speak the **truth** to each other, and render true
and sound judgment in your courts.*
Zechariah 8:16

We have to know the truth to make sound judgments. Otherwise, we are operating on false information, better known as fake news. God is on the side of truth, because He is truth. Satan is the father of lies. It's up to us to choose whom we want to follow, but we better understand the consequences.

Truth always leads to making sound judgments in or out of the court system. Being led astray from the truth always leads us into trouble. We live in one realm or another. The ripple effects for both are huge. Let's avoid trouble! Let's know the truth, speak the truth, and make sound judgments. Let's represent God well.

Do you know the truth so you can speak truthfully and make sound judgments of yourself and others?

PRAYER

Lord Jesus, help me know the truth and let me represent You well.

April 7

THE RIGHT WAY

True worshipers will worship the Father in spirit and **truth***,*
for they are the kind of worshipers the Father seeks.
John 4:23

People like to think they can worship God however they want. In reality, God is very particular in the way He wants us to worship Him, and He has that right. After all, He created the universe with all its stars and galaxies. Then He made our earth as a beautiful planet for us to live. Then He created us in His image, with a heart, mind, and spirit, so we can know Him and communicate with Him.

God wants a personal relationship with each one of us. He wants our spirit to connect with His Spirit. He wants us to come to Him in complete honesty and open our hearts to Him. He wants us to be fully engaged. This is worship in its truest form. This is the worship He seeks.

Is God happy with the way you worship Him? What changes can you make so He is?

PRAYER

Lord Jesus, sometimes I worship You with many distractions competing for Your attention. Help me put them aside so I can be the worshiper You seek.

TRUE FREEDOM

*Then you will know the **truth**,*
*and the **truth** will set you free.*
John 8:32

Jesus spoke these words to the multitudes who were following Him. They were drawn to the truth just like we are. Something about Jesus told them they had found it. They were right.

Knowing Jesus is knowing truth itself. He is the embodiment of truth. Truth is not a theory or a philosophy but is only found in Jesus Christ. He has the power to set us free from sin and give us true freedom as a result. He goes on to say, that "everyone who sins is a slave to sin" (John 8:34). This statement makes our condition without Him even more desperate, because He is the only One who can break the power sin has over us and free us from its everlasting consequences. Jesus gives us true freedom.

Have you allowed Jesus to set you free, so you are no longer a slave to sin?

PRAYER

Lord Jesus, thank You for setting me free so I can live for You.

April 9

THE ONLY WAY

*I am the way and the **truth** and the life.*
No one comes to the Father except through me.
John 14:6

Jesus makes it clear that He is not one way among many ways. He doesn't say that all religions have something good to offer, and you can pick what you want. He doesn't give us any option when it comes to knowing the truth about Him.

The truth is Jesus came to die for our sins and was raised from the dead, so we could be forgiven and spend eternity with Him. He is the only One who can make that claim. Therefore, He is the ONLY way and the ONLY truth, and the ONLY life. His Father won't accept imposters. Choose the ONLY way. Choose Jesus.

Have you made your choice? Do you know how to share this truth with others?

PRAYER

Lord Jesus, so many people think You are just a way to get to Heaven, when in fact, You are the ONLY way. Please help me be bold enough to proclaim it.

April 10

⨏◌

LET HIM IN

*When the Spirit of **truth** comes,*
*he will guide you into all **truth**.*
John 16:13

Before Jesus left this earth and returned to Heaven, He told His confused disciples that He wasn't going to abandon them or leave them to carry on without Him. Even though He would no longer be with them physically, He would send His Spirit to live in and help them. And sure enough, forty days after His resurrection, the Holy Spirit descended on them and many others, and the Church was born. This event is called Pentecost.

Ever since that day, believers have had the same experience. We have received the same Holy Spirit into our hearts, and He guides us into all truth, just like Jesus promised. And Jesus keeps His promise. Now is the time to let Him in.

How much do you allow the Holy Spirit to direct you? How much do you shut Him out?

PRAYER

Lord Jesus, thank You for Your Spirit living in me, help me take advantage of Your wisdom and counsel, which You provide.

WHICH SIDE ARE YOU ON?

*"Everyone on the side
of **truth** listens to me."*
John 18:37

Jesus spoke these words during His trial before Pontius Pilate. Two thousand years later, they remain true. We are bombarded by more voices today than any other time in history; social media has made sure of it. And truth has never been more contested, compromised, hidden, or politicized.

Therefore, it has never been more necessary to know which side we are on. Either we listen to the world around us and fall for its ever-changing perception of truth, or we listen to the One who spoke truth, lived truth, and is truth. Life has never been more fragile, uncertain, insecure, or scary. We better know which side we are on and trust Jesus over all the opposing voices out there.

Do you rely on Jesus and His Word to be the voice of truth in your life?

PRAYER

Lord Jesus, among all the voices in the world today, help me always listen to Yours.

April 12

THE UNIVERSAL QUESTION

*What is **truth**?*
John 18:38

Pontius Pilate asked Jesus that question right before sentencing Him to be crucified. People have been asking the same question ever since. Today the popular answer is—"the truth is anything you want it to be," or "make up your own truth," or "the truth is relative," or "no one knows the truth anyway." If Pontius Pilate had bothered to go and hear Jesus preach or even waited for His answer that day, he would have known that Truth was standing in front of him.

Two thousand years later, Jesus is the same Truth. But like Pontius Pilate, we have to want to hear Him, and we have to accept His answer. Jesus wants everyone to know He is the real Truth.

Are you prepared to defend Jesus as the Truth we all need to know and trust?

PRAYER

Lord Jesus, I want to be prepared to defend You as the Truth. Give me the words and wisdom I need to tell people about You.

April 13

DON'T SUPPRESS IT. EXPRESS IT

The wrath of God is being revealed from heaven
against all the godlessness and wickedness of men
*who suppress the **truth** by their wickedness.*
Romans 1:18

We don't hear much about God's wrath today. We'd much rather hear about His love, grace, and goodness. But the same God who embodies those attributes must also hate any behavior that opposes Him and suppresses the truth about Him. Otherwise, Jesus' death would not have been necessary.

So make no mistake. God's wrath will be revealed against such behavior, because it feeds and encourages the godless living and wicked behavior that threatens every generation. We need to hear more about God's wrath! As believers we need to understand this truth and express it—not suppress it.

Are you as comfortable explaining the validity of God's wrath to people as you are explaining His love?

PRAYER

Lord Jesus, it is much easier to tell people about Your love than about Your wrath. Teach me how to express both.

IT'S NOT WORTH IT

*They exchanged the **truth** of God*
for a lie, and worshiped and served created things
rather than the Creator—who is forever praised.
Romans 1:25

When we don't know the truth, we fall for anything. We are prey to all the lies our culture throws at us. Our priorities become skewed, our values misplaced, and we lose our way. We can be short-sighted, naïve, vulnerable, and gullible!

That's not the path God wants us on. As our Creator, He deserves our worship and allegiance. Nothing and no one else does. Yet we so casually dismiss Him and worship other people and things instead. But at the end of our life, where will that get us? Will we look back with regret that we followed the trends of our culture and missed Him in the process? Don't do it! Don't believe the lies! It's not worth it!

Whom can you come alongside to help decipher the truth from the lies?

PRAYER

Lord Jesus, please show me whom I can show Your truth to amidst all the lies of our culture.

REJOICE

*Love does not delight in evil
but rejoices with the **truth**.*
1 Corinthians 13:6

We live in an upside-down world, a world that calls hate love and lies truth. That explains why people delight in evil. They actually thrive on it and encourage others to join them. We see it live on our screens as mobs gleefully break windows, loot stores, tear down monuments, and threaten the authorities. They justify their actions, because they believe the lie that their rights are more important than the law.

But that behavior is always overshadowed by those who rejoice with the truth. They are the first ones to volunteer to pick up or pay for the mess that others created. And they are eager to do it, because they love God and live by His truth. Join those who rejoice with the truth.

Do people know what side you are on by the way you react to the evil in our midst?

PRAYER

Lord Jesus, help me always stand strong for You.

April 16

NOTHING BUT THE TRUTH

*For we cannot do anything against
the **truth**, but only for the **truth**.*
2 Corinthians 13:8

A s followers of Jesus Christ, we are obligated to support the truth, because He is Truth. His Word is the truth, and there is no changing it or compromising with it. Therefore, everything we listen to, everything we read, everything we study, and everything we say and do must be measured against His standard of truth. As long as we are operating in this reality, we are living in His will for us and we are not only blessing those around us, but we are happier and healthier and more satisfied people as a result. There is only one truth, and nothing will ever destroy it. Let's choose to live by nothing but the truth.

In what areas of your life are you tempted to compromise the truth?

PRAYER

Lord Jesus, help me to live by the truth without compromising it in any area of my life.

April 17

TIME TO GROW UP

---

*Instead, speaking the **truth** in love,*
we will in all things grow up into him
who is the Head, that is, Christ.
Ephesians 4:15

God's goal for every believer is for us to grow and mature in our faith. He wants us to become more and more like Jesus. We are part of His body of believers around the world and therefore, have a responsibility to help and not hinder the rest of the body. We are not to waver or be tossed about by other belief systems or teaching that goes against God or His Church.

Instead, we are to strive to become more and more like Jesus, so we represent Him well. He is our model, and no matter what situation He was in, He always spoke the truth in love. Therefore, so must we. It shows Him and the world around us, we are growing up!

Are you striving to become more like Jesus by speaking the truth in love?

PRAYER

Lord Jesus, help me grow in my relationship with You, so I become more like You in the way I speak and the way I love.

༄༅

BUCKLE YOUR BELT

*Stand firm then, with the belt of **truth**
buckled around your waist.*
Ephesians 6:14

For the Roman soldier, the belt girded his waist and held the rest of his armor together. Paul used his experience of being chained to one of these soldiers during his house arrest in Rome to make this analogy. It gave him the perfect opportunity, and he used it for our benefit.

Believers are to hold fast or stand firm in the truth, which is the gospel message of Jesus' life, death, and resurrection. It is the basis for all that we believe. Therefore, truth holds us together like the soldier's belt held the rest of his armor together. In this world that is governed more by lies than truth, it must be part of our armor as well. In fact, we better not leave home without buckling our belt.

Is the belt of truth fastened tightly around your waist so you are prepared to confront the lies in our culture?

PRAYER

Lord Jesus, help me never leave home without buckling the belt of truth around my waist.

SPREAD THE CURE

*They perish because they refused
to love the **truth** and so be saved.*
2 Thessalonians 2:10

T his has to be one of the saddest sentences in the entire Bible, because unlike other fatal conditions, this one can be cured. God has given every human being the gift of free will, because He is not a dictator who demands our allegiance or a tyrant who controls us. He is a loving God who wants us to love Him in return, so we can know and experience the truth of His love in His Son Jesus Christ. Jesus is the only way we will not perish, but be saved. Otherwise, our sin is a fatal condition, and we will be responsible for not taking the cure. Let's spread the cure.

Whom can you share this truth with so they can know and receive the cure?

PRAYER

Lord Jesus, give me the urgency and the courage to share this truth with someone today.

April 20

BUILD ON THE RIGHT FOUNDATION

*God's household, which is the
church of the living God, the pillar
and foundation of the **truth**.*
1 Timothy 3:15

J esus Christ built His Church on the foundation of Peter's confession of faith in Him as the Christ, the Son of the living God (Matthew 16:16). This declaration by a simple, uneducated fisherman became the dividing line separating Christianity from all the other religions in the world. Jesus called Peter's statement the "rock on which He would build His Church and the gates of hell would not prevail against it" (Matthew 16:18).

As followers of Jesus Christ, we belong to His household and profess the same truth. Satan will always seek to destroy or at least minimize the impact of the Church. But make no mistake, it will always remain the pillar and foundation of the truth.

How are you supporting the Church?

PRAYER

Lord Jesus, help me support your Church as the pillar and foundation of the truth.

HANDLE WITH CARE

*Do your best to present yourself to God as one
approved, a workman who does not need to be
ashamed and who correctly handles the word of **truth**.*
2 Timothy 2:15

As Christians we would all like to hear Jesus say, "Well done, good and faithful servant" (Matthew 25:21) when we stand before Him someday. The choices we make in the meantime can guarantee we will. We don't want to stand before Him ashamed we didn't do more with what He gave us. He gave us the truth in His Word to direct us, and we have no excuse not to handle it with the utmost sincerity, diligence, dependency, faithfulness, and gratitude. We want to be known by Him and by others as people who not only know His truth, but live by His truth. That guarantees His approval and speaks volumes to the people around us. Let's handle His truth with care.

Do you study God's Word diligently so you know the truth and handle it well?

PRAYER

Lord Jesus, help me know Your Word and handle it with care so others want to know it too.

April 22

꧁

BE GENTLE

*Be humble when you are trying to teach
those who are mixed up concerning the **truth**.*
2 Timothy 2:25 (TLB)

The late Christian apologist Ravi Zacharias approached the questions of people who were "mixed up concerning the truth," with the utmost respect and courtesy. He patiently listened to their questions and tried to understand where they were coming from. Then he presented the truth of the gospel clearly and concisely. He gently helped them see Jesus Christ as the only God who does not expect us to come up to Him, like other religions teach. Instead, Jesus came down to us, because we desperately need Him. It's our privilege to teach this great truth, not from a position of pride, but with humility and gratitude that He came for all of us—and then let God do the rest. Be gentle in the way you share God's truth.

How prepared are you to help people who are "mixed up concerning the truth"?

PRAYER

Lord Jesus, please root out any boastful pride, and help me be prepared to share Your truth with humility and respect.

April 23

TIME TO COMMIT

*Always learning but never able
to acknowledge the **truth**.*
2 Timothy 3:7

H ave you ever known anyone who enjoys going to church and even studying the Bible but is not willing to commit to faith in Christ? They seem to want to stay on the fringes and not get too close or involved, because they don't want to give up their so-called freedom or be accountable to anyone else. They justify their thinking by staying on the learning path, instead of getting on the right path.

But there comes a time for all of us when we must make a decision about Jesus Christ. Either He is the truth we all seek or He was a liar, and the Bible is sixty-six books of fake news! We always want to be learning, but we must commit to the truth before it's too late.

Whom can you encourage to find the truth in Jesus Christ today?

PRAYER

Lord Jesus, help me to be ready and willing to help those who are seeking to find the truth in You.

April 24

IS IT REAL?

*If we deliberately keep on sinning after
we have received the knowledge of the **truth**,
no sacrifice for sins is left.*
Hebrews 10:26

When we come to the cross and ask Jesus to forgive our sins, our attitude toward sin changes forever. We are living with the reality of His sacrifice on our behalf and grateful that the burden of our sin is finally lifted. We will continue to sin because our sinful nature will always be with us, but we won't want to. The Holy Spirit in us will make sure of it! It's His job to warn us when we are about to sin and convict us when we do, because sin destroys.

But Jesus paid the price once, and once was enough. If we deliberately keep on sinning, we have to question our salvation and run back to the cross—and this time, make sure it's real.

What is your attitude about sin? How does it line up with God's?

PRAYER

Lord Jesus, help me see sin as You see sin, so I will deliberately avoid it.

FROM THE HEART

Now that you have purified yourselves by obeying the
truth *so that you have sincere love for your brothers,*
love one another deeply, from the heart.
1 Peter 1:22

T he truth purifies us, because it exposes what is false: false thinking, false beliefs, false attitudes, false motives, false actions. Even Christians can buy into this world of fake news. But we are called to live in the truth and obey the truth. It's the only way we can love each other the way Jesus loves us, and the only way we can reach out to others with His love, so they will want to be part of the family.

As believers, it is our responsibility to love our brothers and sisters in the faith, so the Church is vibrant and strong. We are to love them sincerely from our heart, because His love makes the world go 'round and His love makes the Church go 'round.

How are you loving members within your church so it is healthy and strong, and therefore effective in reaching others?

PRAYER

Lord Jesus, help me live in the truth of Your Word, so my love for believers helps strengthen my church, and we can love others with the same love You love us.

April 26

BE CAREFUL WHOM YOU FOLLOW

*Many will follow their shameful ways
and will bring the way of **truth** into disrepute.*
2 Peter 2:2

False teaching is not new. It began when the Church began. Peter addressed it head on and warned early believers not to follow the false teaching permeating their ranks. Thanks to TV and social media, false teaching is bombarding us and threatening the truth of the gospel like never before. We hear all kinds of man-made renditions of God's truth.

As followers of Jesus Christ, we need to be aware and be alarmed. Nothing will take us down faster than denying the truth of God's Word and believing Satan's lie that we can believe anything we want—and that it really doesn't matter anyway. Be careful whom you follow.

Do you know the truth of God's Word enough to be able to detect false teaching when you hear it?

PRAYER

Lord Jesus, help me know Your truth so I can wisely discern what is false.

April 27

PROVE IT

If we claim to have fellowship
with him yet walk in the darkness,
*we lie and do not live by the **truth**.*
1 John 1:6

Have you ever heard the expression, "You may be the only Bible someone ever reads"? That's because our actions often speak louder than our words, and there is simply no greater hypocrisy or poor witness of our faith than saying we are a Christian and living like we aren't.

Jesus expects His followers to be living examples of the truth so that others are drawn to Him as THE Truth. If people don't see that difference in us, they won't see any need for Jesus themselves, and we will be doing Him the greatest disservice. Satan loves to see Christians blend in with his world, because that just keeps more people with him and fewer with Jesus.

How does your life prove your faith in Jesus is real?

PRAYER

Lord Jesus, help my actions for You match my words about You. Help my life prove my faith.

April 28

☙

DON'T BE DECEIVED

*If we claim to be without sin, we deceive
ourselves and the **truth** is not in us.*
1 John 1:8

The hardest thing for any of us to do is to admit we are wrong. But that is the very first thing God requires. Because until we see ourselves the way He sees us—as sinners in need of a Savior—we will be living in the deceit of our own lies. His truth and our lies are not compatible. They cannot coexist.

We must stop making excuses, stop blaming others, and stop procrastinating. We need to stop being deceived and stop deceiving ourselves. We need to call our wrong behavior and our disobedience against God exactly what it is—sin. And then confess it and allow the truth to prevail. Don't be deceived.

How quick are you to confess your sins to God, so He can forgive you and you can move on in truth?

PRAYER

Lord Jesus, help me to keep short accounts with You, because I want to live in Your truth.

April 29

BE CONGRUENT

*Let us not love with words or tongues
but with actions and in **truth**.*
1 John 3:18

S ometimes as Christians we can be obnoxious in our pre-
sentation of the gospel. We can be prideful, self-righteous, indignant, and even forceful. Perhaps it comes from
our own convictions and a genuine desire for people to
know Christ, because we know the benefits. Perhaps it
comes from a sense of urgency, because we know they
might not have another chance. Or perhaps it comes from
our own selfish motive, because we are keeping track of
how many people we have led to Christ.

But whatever the reason, we need to pause and pray
before we speak, because people see Jesus in us before
they hear about Jesus through us.

How sensitive are you when sharing your faith to others?

PRAYER

Lord Jesus, help me always remember to pray before I
speak to someone about You.

April 30

KEEP ON KEEPING ON

*Continue to walk in the **truth**.*
3 John 3

I love to play tennis. One of the cardinal rules of the game is to be consistent. In fact, you will never lose a point, if you get the last ball over the net and keep it in the court.

The same is true for us in our journey of faith. We will never go off the path, if we continue to walk in the truth. The world tempts us to fall for its lies, but we must stay the course to the end. God's Word is our rule book and our line of defense. If we are faithful to read it every day, every day will be guarded by its truth, and God will use it to keep us on the straight path. My prayer has always been, "Lord, help me finish strong," because I don't want to miss a shot. I want to get the last ball over the net. I want to keep on keeping on.

As we come to the end of our study this month, how consistent are you in reading the Bible so you can continue walking in the truth?

PRAYER

Lord Jesus, Your Word is Your direction for my life. Help me walk in its truth until You take me Home

May

HOPE

Our journey of faith gives us **hope**
for today and for the future.

May 1

SOAR

*But those who **hope** in the Lord will
renew their strength. They will soar on wings
like eagles; they will run and not grow weary,
they will walk and not be faint.*
Isaiah 40:31

This is the perfect verse to begin our month and continue our journey of faith, because it so clearly differentiates Christian hope from secular hope. When our hope is in Christ, we draw on His resources as the only living God. We will get weary for sure, because of our physical limitations, but His Word revives, renews, and restores us. And we rise above our circumstances like the eagle I saw on my walk this morning fly above his. We are able to continue our journey with energy, commitment, fortitude, and faith, because the Lord is with us. He is watching and He wants us to soar. Get ready to soar!

Where do you turn when you are weary and need a boost?

PRAYER

Lord Jesus, please help me turn to You first when I feel weary. Don't let me faint; I want to soar.

RESILIENT HOPE

*Though he slay me, yet will I **hope** in him.*
Job 13:15

As I write this, we are in the middle of a global pandemic, and many people are wondering where God is in the midst of it all. Job could have wondered the same thing when he lost everything he had—his health, his wealth, his friends, and his family. But he never lost his hope, because it wasn't wishful-thinking hope, or cross-your-fingers hope or keep-a-positive-attitude hope. It was hope in the same God who had created him and blessed him with everything he had before. Job put his trust in Him, not what He had given him. Therefore, Job's hope was strong enough and resilient enough to weather the hardships, and God blessed him for it.

How resilient is your hope? Is it test worthy because it is in the One who is trustworthy?

PRAYER

Lord Jesus, give me resilient hope that doesn't wonder where You are when trouble comes, but always trusts You when it does.

BE CAREFUL WHAT
YOU HOPE FOR

*A horse is a vain **hope** for deliverance;*
despite all its great strength it cannot save.
Psalm 33:17

My parents owned racehorses when I was growing up in Los Angles, and my favorite activity was going to the track with my dad on Saturday mornings to watch them work out. Their size and strength captivated me, and I dreamed of being the first woman jockey so I could experience it firsthand. Fortunately, that dream didn't work out, but like so many experiences in life, it taught me a valuable lesson—be careful what you hope for.

God wants us to put our hope in Him, because He is the only One who can save us. All other hopes are misleading, because they can bring us momentary satisfaction or pleasure, but they cannot save. Be careful what you hope for.

Is your hope secure in Jesus Christ because He is the only One who has the power to save? What other vain hope do you need to let go of?

PRAYER

Lord Jesus, help me always put my hope in You, because You alone have the power to save.

ARE HIS EYES ON YOU?

*But the eyes of the Lord are
on those who fear him, on those
whose **hope** is in his unfailing love.*
Psalm 33:18

Jesus is a Gentleman. He never forces His way into our life. He waits for our invitation. He waits for us to stop putting our hope in worldly things and come to Him in reverential fear and put our hope and trust in Him. Our invitation gives Him permission to reign supreme in our lives. We become part of His family and as such, He watches over us with His unfailing love.

Think of it! His eyes are always on us, and His unconditional, never-ending, always-with-us love is comforting, guiding, and directing us 24/7. Knowing Jesus loves and cares for us is the real and tangible hope that all believers cling to and live for.

Have you put your hope in Jesus, so He is watching over you with His unfailing love?

PRAYER

Lord Jesus, help me gratefully accept Your watchful care and Your unfailing love and live like I put my hope in You.

May 5

LOOK UP!

Why are you downcast, O my soul?
Why so disturbed within me?
*Put your **hope** in God, for I will yet*
praise him, my Savior and my God.
Psalm 42:5

We are living with unparalleled anxiety, insecurity, depression, and fear because of our ability to know everything that's going on in the world. Social media and the nightly news do not guarantee a good night's sleep!

But instead of giving into the distress it causes, we need to go outside, look up, breathe deeply, and do a mental reset. We need to let go of the hope we may be placing in anything or anyone but God and then just stand there and praise Him. He lifts our soul and renews our hope like nothing and no one else can, because He is our Savior and He is our God. Look up!

What do you do when you feel down or distressed?

PRAYER

Lord Jesus, I can't help but feel the distress these times are creating, but You can help me focus my trust on You. Help me choose to look up and praise You.

May 6

A GOOD REFLECTION

May those who fear you rejoice
when they see me, for I have put
*my **hope** in your word.*
Psalm 119:74

C hristians always need each other, but never more so
than now. The world is in chaos. Yet we know that
will be the case as we approach the second coming of
Jesus Christ. As that time gets closer, we are to encourage
each other. We are to reflect His love, we are to rejoice
with each other in our singing and our worship, and we
are to study His Word more faithfully and diligently than
ever before.

In the midst of the chaos, the Bible is the only source of
true hope, because it tells us what we need to know about
what's going to happen next. Therefore, we need to stick
together and strengthen each other so we can share our
hope with the world.

Do your friends and family rejoice when they see you,
because you have been in the Word of God and your
countenance and attitude reflect it?

PRAYER

Lord Jesus, help me spend time in Your Word every day,
so I reflect You to those around me and everyone I meet.

May 7

WORTH THE WAIT

I wait for the Lord, my soul waits,
*and in his word I put my **hope**.*
Psalm 130:5

S ometimes God seems so silent and we can't help but
wonder why. Where is He? Does He see what I am going
through? Does He care? These questions can plague all of
us, because waiting is hard and we're not used to it. After
all, this is the instant generation. We are used to everything
from Instagram to Instant Pots.

And yet God refuses to adjust to our timetable and instead,
we wait. We wait because we know He is with us, we know
He sees what we are going through, and we know He
cares. So we hunker down with our Bible and wait. And
then it comes—a word, a sentence, a promise that gets
our attention and gives us hope like nothing else can.

What do you do when you're impatient for God to act?

PRAYER

Lord Jesus, please help me turn to Your Word while I wait
for You to act, because it's the best place to wait.

May 8

BE BLESSED
---

*Blessed is he . . . whose **hope**
is in the Lord his God.*
Psalm 146:5

The word *blessed* can mean to make happy. We all want to be happy. No one wants to be unhappy. So what is the secret of happiness? The world tells us that happiness is found in a great vacation or the perfect mate or the right career or an early retirement.

But the Bible says hope is not found in any of these temporary ambitions or desires, but in God, the Maker of Heaven and earth. And why wouldn't we find happiness with Him? After all, He created us to be happy. Adam and Eve were in total bliss with Him in the Garden of Eden, until Satan came along and spoiled their happiness and ours. Thank God for Jesus, in Him we find true happiness.

How are you being fooled by the world into hoping it can bring you happiness?

PRAYER

Lord Jesus, help my hope to be in You, so I am blessed and therefore happy,

BE A DELIGHT

The Lord delights in those who fear him,
*who put their **hope** in his unfailing love.*
Psalm 147:11

C an you think of anything better than God delighting in you? You would think we would get lost in the vastness of the universe and go unnoticed among the billions of people on earth. But no! God doesn't lose track of any of us.

God is grieved by those who reject Him, and He is delighted with those who fear Him, or have reverence for Him, because they believe in Him. Those who reject Him are without hope, because He is our only hope in a world that is desperate for it. But those who believe have unending hope, because it is based on His unfailing love. We often thank God for delighting us by answering our prayers, but we should also thank Him that we can delight Him.

How are you delighting God by putting your hope in His unfailing love?

PRAYER

Lord Jesus, I would like nothing more than to delight You! Help me do so by putting my hope in nothing less than Your unfailing love.

DON'T PUT IT OFF

Hope *deferred makes the heart sick.*
Proverbs 13:12

We can spend our whole life wanting the wrong things, going after the wrong things, and hoping for the wrong things. The world tries to make us short-sighted and misguided. And we suffer in the process.

We were created in the image of God so we can know Him and know His plans for us. He created us to be tuned into Him, so He can communicate His hopes for us—to us. But we can get so sidetracked and waste so many years trying to do life our way, that we often deal with unnecessary heartache as a result. Augustine had it right when he said our hearts are restless until they find their rest in Thee. Don't put it off any longer. Hope in God!

How are you putting your hope in other people or things instead of God? With what result?

PRAYER

Lord Jesus, help me do my heart a favor and put my hope in You.

May 11

CLAIM YOUR FUTURE

---

*There is surely a future **hope** for you,*
*and your **hope** will not be cut off.*
Proverbs 23:18

E veryone is curious about their future. It keeps palm readers and fortune tellers in business. And if they want to stay in business, they better predict a good future, at least one with some hope. But even then, that prediction could vary from one source to another, and hope is dashed. No wonder God's Word condemns these practices. (Leviticus 19:26)

For Christians, our future is secure, because our hope is in Jesus Christ. It will never be cut off, because He will never change. Christians are to set the example of this hope, so unbelievers turn away from their futile attempts to know their future and turn to Christ as the only One who does. Claim your future in Jesus.

How do you condone palm reading and fortune telling by making light of them instead of condemning them as the evil practices they are?

PRAYER

Lord Jesus, help me see evil where You see evil and then have Your response.

May 12

GOD KNOWS BEST

For I know the plans I have for you, declares the Lord,
plans to prosper you and not to harm you, plans to
*give you **hope** and a future.*
Jeremiah 29:11

Have you ever felt like God is against you, that He is not that interested in the school you go to, or who you marry, or the career you choose, or all the other major decisions you make? This verse is reassuring and well known among believers because it tells us the exact opposite. It tells us God has a plan for our life. It tells us He didn't just create us and leave us on our own to figure out what we are supposed to do. But He created us with unique gifts and talents that best fit His plan. We save ourselves a lot of grief if we ask Him to lead us into His plans, instead of floundering around on our own. After all, God knows best.

What plans are you making that you need to stop and consult Him about, so you know you are on the right path?

PRAYER

Lord Jesus, help me consult You with my plans so my hope and my future are aligned with Yours.

GROW IN SUFFERING

We know that suffering produces perseverance;
*perseverance, character; and character, **hope**.*
Romans 5:3-4

Believers can look at suffering differently than non-be-lievers, because we know that God uses it for good. I can look back on my life and say with confidence and gratitude, that I learned more about God and about myself during times of suffering, than I did when everything was going great.

In times of suffering we learn to hang on and persevere. We learn how much we need God. We develop backbone, grit, wisdom, tenacity, strength, and other values we might not have had otherwise. Suffering shapes our character and makes us more like Jesus. That gives us hope, because we know it is only temporary and someday, we will be with Him.

How do you react in times of suffering? Do others see you use it as an opportunity to grow in your faith and want to do the same?

PRAYER

Lord Jesus, no one has ever suffered like You suffered. Help me trust You to use my suffering for Your sake and Your glory.

May 14

A GUARANTEED HOPE

*And **hope** does not disappoint us, because
God has poured out his love into our hearts
by the Holy Spirit, whom he has given us.
Romans 5:5*

Hope for the believer does not disappoint because it is founded on the truth of the gospel. Jesus came and died for our sins and rose from the dead to prove to the world that He is the promised Messiah and the only Savior. This hope can never disappoint, because it means our sins are forgiven. And even though we will die in this life, we will be resurrected just like He was, and live with Him forever in the next. Rather than disappoint, this hope energizes us, motivates us, equips us, and thrives in us, because it is constantly being fed by God's Spirit pouring His love into our hearts. His hope comes with an eternal guarantee.

Is your hope based on the foundational truth of the gospel or is it based on unfounded optimism?

PRAYER

Lord Jesus, help me put my hope in You, because it's the only hope that comes with an eternal guarantee.

ALL NEW

---

*In **hope** that the creation itself
will be liberated from its bondage
and brought into the glorious freedom
of the children of God.*
Romans 8:20-21

Humans aren't the only ones groaning under the weight of sin. All of creation groans as well. But when Jesus returns, it will be liberated and join the freedom that God's children will enjoy in the new heavens and the new earth (Rev 21), where there is no more sin and no more suffering and no more death. And we will experience creation like Adam and Eve did prior to their fatal act of disobedience. We cannot imagine the glorious freedom and the sheer beauty, but even the universe we live in and the animal kingdom we enjoy are looking forward to it.

Whom will you share this hope with about Jesus' return?

PRAYER

Lord Jesus, help me share this great hope with someone who needs to hear that when You return, everything will be made new.

May 16

HOPE REALIZED

*But **hope** that is seen is no hope at all.*
Romans 8:24

The trouble with hope is that it is so elusive, evasive, hard to describe, and even harder to hold onto. But that's exactly what makes Christian hope so beautiful and life changing. Even though we can't see it, touch it, or feel it like we do when we are hoping to buy something we want, our hope is solid, because it is based on the proven fact of the gospel.

The gospel of Jesus Christ has never changed, gone out of style, or become irrelevant. We are saved by faith, but hope accompanies salvation, because it changes our perspective. We live and die differently. We trust Jesus because of what He did for us and what He is going to do for us. Hope in Jesus is hope realized.

How would you explain the difference between the world's hope and the hope we have in Christ?

PRAYER

Lord Jesus, our world feels hopeless right now, help me to share the hope I have because of You.

PATIENT HOPE

*But if we **hope** for what we do not
yet have, we wait for it patiently.*
Romans 8:25

Who doesn't remember being a kid and counting down the days until Christmas? I remember the year I wanted a life size doll, and wanting it so badly, it was all I could think about. I was anything but patient as I waited for Santa to deliver it.

Waiting for something to materialize can be frustrating, irritating, and disappointing, because there's always the possibility it won't happen. But believers can wait patiently, because we know we will receive what has been promised, and we know it will be worth the wait. Jesus has delivered on every promise except one—His return—and we can wait patiently and with hope, because we know His return will happen.

How does Jesus' promise to return affect the way you live each day?

PRAYER

Lord Jesus, help me use each day wisely as I patiently wait for You to return.

May 18

JOYFUL HOPE

*Be joyful in **hope**,*
patient in affliction, faithful in prayer.
Romans 12:12

For the Christian, joy is not in what happens to us, but in what has already happened for us. It is different than happiness which depends on our circumstances to make us happy. Joy wells up from within us regardless of our circumstances because of the Source.

We have God's Holy Spirit living in us to supply what we cannot supply for ourselves. He makes us joyful when there is no reasonable reason to be joyful. He gives us patience in affliction when there is no reasonable reason to be patient. And He nudges us to pray when we don't feel like it or there's every excuse not to. Joy is the trademark of every true believer. How can it not be?

How have you experienced joyful hope even in a difficult situation and whom can you share it with?

PRAYER

Lord Jesus, thank You for Your joy that springs up from within me even when there shouldn't be any joy. Help me be quick to share You as the Source of my joy.

May 19

BE ENCOURAGED

*For everything that was written
in the past was written to teach us, so that
through endurance and the encouragement
of the Scriptures we might have **hope**.*
Romans 15:4

Everything we need to know about life and death is carefully written out for us in the sixty-six books of the Bible. It comes to us directly from God. It is our manual for living. Every word written by every contributing author is inspired by His Holy Spirit (2 Timothy 3:16).

Today, the Bible remains the bestseller of all time and many homes boast of having several. But unfortunately, it is seldom taken off the shelf, let alone read. Yet there is no book ever written or could ever be written that gives us more encouragement to endure the ups and downs of life or produce the hope we have, because it tells us the best is yet to come. Be encouraged. Read your Bible.

How much do you depend on the Bible to give you the wisdom, encouragement and hope you need to live by?

PRAYER

Lord Jesus, help me be disciplined in my study of Your Word for the encouragement, endurance, and hope You want me to have each day.

❦

BE FILLED

*May the God of **hope** fill you with all joy and peace
as you trust in him, so that you may overflow with
hope by the power of the Holy Spirit.*
Romans 15:13

Only God can give us hope in a world that feels increasingly hopeless, a country that seems to be losing its way, and families that are struggling to stay together. Yet we turn to so many other solutions before turning to Him. Sometimes it takes a crisis to force us to realize that our hope is not in governments, political leaders, or just hoping things will work out.

Sometimes the only thing we can do is to let go of our own solutions and trust God for His. When we lean into Him, we can take a deep breath and feel His joy and peace fill us up. Our hope is renewed, because the Holy Spirit reminds us that He is on the Throne, controlling the world's future and ours. Be filled.

What situation are you in today where you need to trust God like never before? Will you?

PRAYER

Lord Jesus, please help me remember that You are on the Throne and I can trust You.

May 21

DON'T BE SHORT-SIGHTED

*If only for this life we have **hope** in Christ,
we are to be pitied more than all men.*
1 Corinthians 15:19

Christians have the advantage of knowing that this life is not all there is. It is not the end of our story. In fact, this life is just a blip on the screen of eternity. So it only stands to reason that our faith is always looking forward to our next life in Heaven, because we will be there forever.

That is our greatest hope, because it is God's ultimate promise to all who believe in Him and receive the gift of salvation through Jesus Christ. Worldly hope is limited to this world but our future extends beyond this world. Jesus went ahead of us to prepare the way, so we know where we are going (John 14:1-3). Don't be short-sighted!

How are you being short-sighted by limiting your hope to the things of this world rather than on God's promise for believers after death?

PRAYER

Lord Jesus, help me not be short-sighted and limit my hope in You for this life only, but help me look beyond this life to the next with great hope, because You are there.

May 22

BEFORE AND AFTER

Remember that at that time you were separate from Christ . . . without **hope** *and without God in the world.*
Ephesians 2:12

Before we come to Christ for salvation, we are separated from Christ. We are outside God's family. We live for ourselves and have no moral standard or accountability. Our hearts are hard toward the things of God, and our understanding is dark because Satan controls it. Our hope is limited to the things of the world rather than the things of God, because we choose to stay there.

But after we come to Christ, we realize His blessings—that we are chosen, adopted, redeemed, forgiven, included in His plans and purpose, and sealed forever by His Holy Spirit (Ephesians 1:1-14). Life is never the same. Don't miss the 'after'!

How would you describe your life before you met Jesus?

PRAYER

Lord Jesus, help my life with You be so appealing to unbelievers, they will want You too.

GO FOR THE GLORY

*Christ in you, the **hope** of glory.*
Colossians 1:27

It's tempting to crave the world's glory. Our human nature likes to be recognized. We like to be honored. We like to stand out. We like to be known for our successes and accomplishments and rewarded accordingly. But there's glory here on earth and there's glory in Heaven.

Without Christ, any glory we hope for will be temporary and limited to our present life. And any glory believers experience here will pale in comparison to the eternal glory that awaits us in Heaven. Jesus sent His Spirit to live in us to expand our hope to what He has in store for us. Let's forego any glory we are seeking here and go for His!

How are you settling for the world's glory and passing up the glory that awaits you in Heaven?

PRAYER

Lord Jesus, help me give You any glory I receive here on earth as I look forward to experiencing Your glory in Heaven.

OUR ONLY HOPE

*We continually remember before our God
and Father . . . your endurance inspired
by **hope** in our Lord Jesus Christ.*
1 Thessalonians 1:3

Nothing makes us endure hardship more than hope. We hope for a phone call. We hope for a job. We hope for a cure. We're always hoping for something. And hope inspires us to keep on enduring.

Paul was grateful for this church in Thessalonica, because they believed Jesus' promise to return. Hope in that promise kept them going, and hope in that promise has kept believers going ever since. In a world that is getting more dangerous by the day, because it insists on living apart from Christ and therefore apart from this hope, it is our privilege to tell people He is coming back. He is our only hope, and He will help us endure until He returns.

Whom can you share this promise with to give them hope to endure?

PRAYER

Lord Jesus, in a world without hope, You are our hope. Please help me share You with others today.

WHAT ARE YOU WORKING FOR?

For this we labor and strive,
*that we have put our **hope** in the living God,*
who is the Savior of all men.
1 Timothy 4:10

We were born to work. God worked to create the universe and this world we live in, and He gave Adam and Eve work to do in the Garden. Work makes us feel good about ourselves and useful to others. Hope is part of the work we do. We hope to get good grades, we hope to make the team, we hope to graduate, we hope to please our boss, we hope to manage our affairs well enough to retire.

God wants us to work, and He wants us to do well in our work. But primarily He wants us to work for Him in whatever work we do and whatever environment we are in, because He is the Savior of all men. He wants everyone to know it and put their hope in Him.

How can the work you do show people that you really work for God?

PRAYER

Lord Jesus, help me show others that I primarily work for You in everything I do, so they will see the benefits and want to work for You too.

DON'T WASTE YOUR HOPE

Command those who are rich in this present world not
*to be arrogant nor to put their **hope** in wealth.*
1 Timothy 6:17

Jesus said it was harder for a rich man to believe than a poor man. In fact He said it was harder for a camel to go through the eye of a needle than for a rich man to enter the kingdom of Heaven (Matthew 19:24).

Paul knew this firsthand. He had come from a wealthy family and was on that track himself when his world was turned upside down. He knew how easy it was to hope in money and wealth and be arrogant as a result. So he passed this command on to Timothy to pass on to the church—don't waste your hope on money. It could lose its value any day. Instead put your hope in God. He controls all things, and that will never change. Don't waste your hope.

What are you putting your hope in that could change, instead of in God, who will never change?

PRAYER

Lord Jesus, help me not waste my hope on anything in this world that is always subject to change. Keep my hope on You, because You never change.

RESTING HOPE

*A faith and knowledge resting on the **hope**
of eternal life, which God, who does not lie,
promised before the beginning of time.*
Titus 1:2

God wants us to put our hope in Him because He offers us eternal life. This hope is as old as time itself. He wants everyone in every generation to know it, study it, and believe it, because it will guide everything we do, from the way we live to the way we die. When we know with absolute certainty that we will live with Him forever, we will live differently than we've ever lived before. This world is stressful, uncertain, and scary, but we can rest in Jesus, because He has our future all planned out, and we are secure in Him. Make sure your hope is resting hope.

Are the stresses of this world wearing you out? Rest in Jesus. He gives us the hope of eternal life now.

PRAYER

Lord Jesus, help me find my rest in You, because You give me the hope of eternal life beginning now.

May 28

BLESSED HOPE

*While we wait for the blessed **hope***—
the glorious appearing of our great
God and Savior, Jesus Christ.
Titus 2:13

If you are a believer, there is no greater event to look forward to than the return of Jesus Christ. If you are not a believer, there is no event you should dread more than the return of Jesus Christ. But if you aren't a believer yet, why not ask yourself, what have I got to lose? And then choose to take Jesus at His Word and accept His offer of salvation for your sins. You have nothing to lose but eternity in Hell.

The truth is the Bible speaks more about the dangers of Hell than the ecstasy of Heaven, because people would rather put their hopes in this world than in the blessed hope of His return. But at the end of the day, only one hope is blessed. Choose the blessed hope.

How does your life reflect your thoughts about the promise of Jesus' return?

PRAYER

Lord Jesus, help me give Your return serious thought and then live like I'm looking forward to it.

May 29

SECURE HOPE

*We have this **hope** as an anchor*
for the soul, firm and secure.
Hebrews 6:19

Living in the Pacific Northwest, we have always loved boating. But it can be dangerous! I remember a particularly memorable time when we rafted two boats together and anchored for the night. A wind came up, our anchor came loose, and we woke up just in time to avoid crashing into a huge cliff of rocks. If our hope had been in that anchor holding us, we could have drowned.

We need an anchor that will hold us firm and secure no matter how fierce the wind or deep the water or huge the obstacle. We need Jesus. He is our secure hope.

Whom or what are you depending on to keep you secure when the winds come up in your life?

PRAYER

Lord Jesus, help me to trust You to hold me firm and secure in this insecure world.

May 30

PROFESS YOUR HOPE

*Let us hold unswervingly to the **hope** we profess, for he who promised is faithful.*
Hebrews 10:23

In this world of unprecedented social tension, divided politics, lawlessness and fear, Christians are the silent minority when we need to be the vocal majority. We need to speak up for what we believe instead of catering to those who don't believe. We need to stand up for God, His Word, and His Son. We need to spread the good news of salvation through Him to a world that is dying without Him.

This is no time to cower and hide. It's time to stand up, speak out, and be proud of what we believe and why. If we don't, we are acting like we don't trust the One we profess to believe. And yet He has always been faithful, and He will be faithful now. Profess your hope.

Whom are you afraid to share your faith with and why?

PRAYER

Lord Jesus, You have always been faithful to me, help me trust Your faithfulness to speak up and speak out for You now.

BE PURE

Dear friends . . . we know that when
he appears, we shall be like him,
for we shall see him as he is.
Everyone who has this **hope** *in him*
purifies himself, just as he is pure.
1 John 3:2-3

The greatest event that will ever take place on planet earth is the return of Jesus Christ. The whole world is reeling and groaning under the weight of sin. Only His return will change it, because He is returning to make things right.

Every other promise in the Bible about Jesus has been fulfilled. With an accuracy record like that, we know this one will be fulfilled too. It is the great hope of every believer that keeps us going in our journey of faith. It's the hope that overrides all the bad news and aligns our thinking with His. It's the hope that makes us live for Him and not ourselves. It's the hope that purifies us in an impure world. Look forward to Jesus' return and be pure.

How often do you think about Jesus' return and how does it affect your life?

PRAYER

Lord Jesus, help me think more about Your return so I am living for You in the meantime.

June

STRENGTH

❧

We need God's **strength**
on our journey of faith.

June 1

STAND UP AND FIGHT

*Be **strong** and courageous. Do not be afraid or terrified because of them, for the Lord your God goes with you; he will never leave you nor forsake you.*
Deuteronomy 31:6

It takes blatant courage to stand against those who oppose us. The Israelites were terrified to enter the land God had promised them, because it was occupied by many different peoples. But God had promised it to them, and God keeps His promises, so He appointed Joshua to lead them in and claim it.

As we continue our journey of faith, we find ourselves surrounded by many enemies who oppose our faith in God and basically want Him removed from our culture. Joshua's words to the Israelites are just as true for us as they were for them. We cannot shrink back and let the enemy win. We must stand up and fight and reclaim the land He has given us.

Are you standing strong in your faith in a world that is increasingly hostile to God?

PRAYER

Lord Jesus, help me live with courage in our hostile world, because I know You are with me.

TIME TO CHOOSE

*It is not by **strength** that one prevails; those who
oppose the Lord will be shattered.*
1 Samuel 2:9-10

God appointed Samuel to establish the rule of kingship early in Israel's history. It was surrounded by enemies then, just as it is today. Samuel held the Israelites accountable to their unique position and God's covenant agreement with them—He would bless them if they obeyed Him.

The same holds true for us today. We are only entitled to God's blessings when we put our faith and trust in Him and live in obedience to His Word. We have to choose which side we are on. Either we are with God and have His eternal protection, or we oppose Him and lose it. If you haven't made your choice, now is the time.

Have you made your choice to stand with God? If not, what are you waiting for?

PRAYER

Lord Jesus, help me stand firm with You. I want Your blessings in my life.

SUPERNATURAL STRENGTH

*It is God who arms me with **strength**
and makes my way perfect.*
Psalm 18:32

Have you ever heard the expression, "you just need to pull yourself up by your bootstraps?" If you haven't, don't worry, God hasn't either. In fact, it is totally contrary to His Word and what He wants to do for us. Unfortunately, we buy into this kind of self-help type thinking and feel like a failure if we can't help ourselves.

But God never intended for us to handle the stresses of life alone. He is there to help us when we can't get up. In fact, it's those desperate times when we're at the end of our own strength that He shows up in the most unexpected ways. He strengthens us with His supernatural strength that defies our own.

Where do you need His supernatural strength today? Will you ask Him for it?

PRAYER

Lord Jesus, help me never be too proud to ask for Your strength when I am at the end of mine.

June 4

RETURNING AS KING

*Who is this King of Glory? The Lord **strong** and mighty,
the Lord mighty in battle.*
Psalm 24:8

Jesus came the first time as a helpless baby, but He's coming the second time as the triumphant and reigning King. He is coming to defeat His enemies—those that have always opposed Him—and bring peace to this earth.

As the world is embroiled in "wars and rumors of wars" (Matthew 24:6) with no end in sight, we can look forward to this time when Jesus says, "Enough is enough!" We can look forward to the time when the words of this beloved Christmas carol are fulfilled: "Joy to the World the Lord is come, let earth receive her King." Jesus may have been born in a manger, but He is returning as King. In the meantime, He is strong enough to fight our battles.

What battle do you need to allow King Jesus to fight for you today?

PRAYER

Lord Jesus, help me bow to You as the King of Glory and trust You to fight my battles.

THE BEST SOLUTION

*Wait for the Lord; be **strong***
and take heart and wait for the Lord.
Psalm 27:14

Waiting is hard for all of us, whether we believe in God or not. The difference is that unbelievers are waiting for themselves, or someone else, to figure out the solution and come to their aid. They are depending on human strength and human solutions and they work hard to make it happen.

Believers, on the other hand, are depending on God to intervene and give them His strength while waiting for His solution. Doing life with Jesus is much more secure, and I might add, more fun. He is our companion and guide. He gives us courage and patience while we wait. With Him by our side, waiting is much less stressful, because we know He will lead us to the best solution.

What problem are you waiting to be resolved and whose strength are you depending on while you wait, yours or God's?

PRAYER

Lord Jesus, help me turn to You to solve this problem and give me Your strength while I wait.

OUR SURE DEFENSE

*The Lord is my **strength** and my shield;*
my heart trusts in him and I am helped.
Psalm 28:7

In ancient Israel, the king protected his people like a shield. Jesus is our King and He protects our heart like a shield. What a comfort knowing that nothing comes to us that doesn't go through Him first. We need His strength to fight our battles every day. We need His protection from hard situations, hurtful relationships, and harmful choices.

Paul used the shield, of the Roman guard he was chained to, as an illustration of how our shield of faith protects us from the flaming arrows of the evil one (Ephesians 6:16). Satan seeks to destroy, but Jesus is our sure defense. We can trust Him.

What situation are you in where you simply need to trust Jesus to protect you?

PRAYER

Lord Jesus, You are my King and my sure defense, help me trust You and be strengthened.

June 7

A MIGHTY FORTRESS

*The Lord is the **strength** of his people,*
a fortress of salvation for his anointed one.
Psalm 28:8

What do you think of when you think of a fortress? A fort with a huge wall or a castle with a deep moat? Both provide a barrier of safety for those inside.

Salvation from sin is God's barrier of protection for all believers. We are safe in Him because we belong to Him and nothing can harm us apart from Him. He stands guard over our lives and gives us His strength to live the life Jesus won for us on the cross. We are His anointed, and He is our mighty fortress. It's the best place to be.

Are you safe behind His fortress because you belong to Jesus?

PRAYER

Lord Jesus, thank You for the safety I have in You. Help me live out my salvation as one of Your anointed.

June 8

HOPE IN THE LORD

*Be **strong** and take heart,*
all you who hope in the Lord.
Psalm 31:24

Our world is in turmoil, and even believers can become discouraged. But people are watching us to see how we will respond. Will we react in a way that mimics theirs and therefore, not offer any better solution? Or will we react in a way that shows off God's strength, and they will want it for themselves?

I remember being drawn to God at an early age by watching my friend's mom deal with a difficult situation. I saw her strength, fortitude, and resolve as she quietly, but consistently, trusted God and never lost hope. She was a living example for an impressionable young girl.

We may become discouraged now and then, but we won't lose heart when our hope is in Him, because He gives us His strength not to lose heart.

Are you depending on God to strengthen you and give you hope in a difficult situation? Take heart, He will give it to you.

PRAYER

Lord Jesus, help me draw my strength from You and hope in You, so I won't lose heart.

EVER-PRESENT HELP

*God is our refuge and **strength**,*
an ever-present help in trouble.
Psalm 46:1

Ever-present is the key to understanding this verse. We can seek refuge in something positive, like a career or recreation, or in something negative, like drugs or alcohol. We can become strong by working out and getting fit. But both these sources for refuge and strength depend on variables like job security, health, and finances. They can work in our favor one minute and fail us the next.

But God is the one refuge and the one source of strength that never changes. We can be tempted to call home or phone a friend, but He is the one constant in a constantly changing world. He is our only ever-present help in trouble.

Do you go to the phone or to the Throne when you are in trouble?

PRAYER

Lord Jesus, thank You for always being there for me. Help me do You the honor of going to You first.

THE SAME GOD

*The God of Israel gives power
and **strength** to his people.*
Psalm 68:35

The tiny nation of Israel has survived two millennia of countless attacks and wars with her enemies. She could have been wiped off the face of the earth a long time ago, but she remains. Today she is a thriving and prosperous nation and a major contributor to the world's economy. People scratch their heads and wonder why.

But believers know. Israel has survived against all odds, because she is God's chosen nation to make Himself known to the world. We have the Jewish people to thank for His Word and His Son, our Savior Jesus Christ. Israel's God is our God, and He gives us the same strength He gave this tiny nation to survive and thrive in a dangerous world.

What do you need God's power and strength for today? Will you ask Him for it?

PRAYER

Lord Jesus, help me come to You for Your power and strength, instead of trusting my own.

THE RIGHT PATH

*Blessed are those whose **strength** is in you,*
who have set their hearts on pilgrimage.
Psalm 84:5

Life is a spiritual journey whether we realize it or not. God created us with a special place in our heart that only He can fill. Sometimes it takes a lifetime of trying to fill it with something else before we realize it.

My paternal grandfather was a brilliant young man, graduating from Yale while still in his teens. But he wasted the next fifty years of his life in pursuit of all the wrong pleasures. Desperate and alone, he reconnected with the family when I was a teenager. By that time, he had realized his folly and surrendered his life to Christ. I was the beneficiary. His pilgrimage was ending; mine was beginning. He helped me get started on the right path.

Whom can you help get started on the right path?

PRAYER

Lord Jesus, help me be tuned into You so I can help someone start their pilgrimage with You.

June 12

KEEP MOVING

---

*They go from **strength** to **strength**,*
till each appears before God in Zion.
Psalm 84:7

When we come to God through a personal relationship with Jesus Christ, we are no longer our own. His Holy Spirit is now living in us, and He becomes our coach, teacher, mentor, and motivator to make us more and more like Jesus.

We can tune out the Holy Spirit for sure, but He is there nonetheless. It is His job to lead us forward in our journey of faith—to remind us to study the Bible and nudge us to pray so our faith becomes stronger and stronger. He helps us move forward with God, from strength to strength, so when we meet Him face to face, we are not ashamed or embarrassed, but confident and comfortable, because we know Him well.

Are you tuning in to the Holy Spirit to help you grow from strength to strength, or are you tuning Him out?

PRAYER

Lord Jesus, help me tune in to You and move forward in my faith, from strength to strength.

June 13

GO TO THE STRENGTH

Your arm is endued with power;
*your hand is **strong**, your right hand exalted.*
Psalm 89:13

It takes hard work and discipline to make our bodies strong, but it's a good feeling when we make the effort. The work pays off. We have more energy and stamina. Our mind is sharper. Our thinking is clear. We are more alert, aware, interested, and motivated to tackle life with focus and enthusiasm.

God made our bodies incredibly strong and durable, but no matter how strong we think we are, our strength will always be limited. That's why we need His strength. He doesn't need to work at it. It's just part of who He is.

Whose strength are you depending on, yours or His?

PRAYER

Lord Jesus, help me work to make my body strong but depend on You to make my faith strong.

DRESS FOR THE OCCASION

*She is clothed with **strength** and dignity;*
she can laugh at the days to come.
Proverbs 31:25

This verse reminds me of my oldest daughter, who has suffered with a chronic illness since her teens. We thought her health issues would prevent her from having children, but God had a different idea—twin boys at forty. Although her health remains a constant threat, she has three things going for her: her faith, her resilience, and her sense of humor.

No one goes through life without challenges and hardship, but we all choose how we respond. Faith in God equips us with His strength to bounce back or be resilient to the hard things life throws at us. A sense of humor gives us the right perspective. Life is hard. We should dress for the occasion.

How do you respond to the challenges in your life?

PRAYER

Lord Jesus, help me deal with the challenges in my life in a way that honors You and encourages others.

NUMBER ONE DOC

Strengthen *the feeble hands,*
steady the knees that give way.
Isaiah 35:3

Today's medical technology is amazing. We can replace any of our body joints that give out on us. I have friends that have had double knee replacements and are back playing tennis. But not all such surgeries are successful. We can't depend on a twenty, forty, or sixty percent success rate to make us strong for life.

We need the 100% success rate that only Jesus offers. He is the Great Physician and the only One who can strengthen our feeble hands and steady our knees when we are at the end of our strength and have more life to live. Go to Jesus. The best part is, His services are free, you don't have to wait, and you won't need a second opinion.

What does it take for you to go to Jesus for the strength you need?

PRAYER

Lord Jesus, help me turn to You before I become weak and feeble, so I have Your continued strength.

June 16

RECHARGE YOUR BATTERY

*He gives **strength** to the weary and
increases the power of the weak.
Isaiah 40:29*

G OD is my POWERCORD is written on the mouse pad next to my computer. It's a great reminder when I am feeling weary and brain dead that He is here cheering me on. I just need to stop and let His Spirit do the thinking for me.

Maybe you are tired for different reasons. Maybe you are exhausted from homeschooling your kids during a pandemic, or tired from taking care of your elderly parents, or tired from working long hours at a job you're not crazy about. But whatever is making you tired, just remember, God is with you ready to infuse His strength into you. Take a break in His Word and feel His power. Recharge your battery!

What do you do when you need to recharge your battery?

PRAYER

Lord Jesus, You are the power source I need. Help me go to Your Word to recharge.

SAFETY IN A SCARY WORLD

*O Lord, my **strength** and my fortress,*
my refuge in times of distress.
Jeremiah 16:19

B eing in the middle of a global pandemic causes wide-spread anxiety and fear, even among our children. My niece's five-year-old daughter was told she couldn't play in her friend's yard, because the virus "sticks on everything." She replied, "I am so glad Jesus keeps me safe."

There is no other place of refuge in this uncertain and scary world than Jesus Christ. How comforting it is to know, with the same assurance this little girl had, that we are safe when we belong to Him.

Where do you seek comfort and security in this uncertain and scary world?

PRAYER

Lord Jesus, help me seek safety in You alone, because You are my only refuge in times of distress.

June 18

UNTIL HE RETURNS

But I have prayed for you, Simon,
that your faith may not fail. And when you
*have turned back, **strengthen** your brothers.*
Luke 22:32

There is nothing more comforting in this troubled world than knowing that Jesus is praying for us, just as He prayed for Peter. That was His promise to us in His High Priestly Prayer during His Last Supper here on earth (John 17). He knew the challenging world He was leaving to His disciples. He knew the Great Commission (Matthew 28:19-20) to spread the good news of salvation through Him would be met with ridicule, rejection, persecution, and death.

Jesus also knew it would be no different today, two thousand years later. And so He prayed. He prayed for Peter that night and He prays for us today, because His commission continues until He returns.

Who needs your prayers that their faith will not fail?

PRAYER

Lord Jesus, show me whom I can pray for today, for You to strengthen their faith.

AT THE END OF THE DAY

Strengthening *the disciples
and encouraging them to
remain true to the faith.*
Acts 14:22

B elievers have never needed each other more so than now. As I'm writing this, we continue to be in partial lockdown due to Covid-19. And while protestors are allowed to protest in our streets, Christians are not allowed to meet in our churches. It's time we let our voices be heard so we can get back together again.

God knows we need the companionship of being with like-minded people, and He encourages us to do so (Hebrews 10:25). We need to stand up and worship God—together. We need to sing the great hymns of our faith—together. We need to kneel and pray—together. We need to strengthen each other in our faith, because at the end of the day, that is all we have.

How do you stay connected with other believers when you can't be together physically?

PRAYER

Lord Jesus, help me be available to listen, encourage, and pray with other believers.

June 20

ONE STEP AT A TIME

He (Abraham) did not waver through unbelief
*regarding the promise of God, but was **strengthened***
in his faith and gave glory to God.
Romans 4:20

Indecision is a horrible state of mind. We vacillate between one decision and another. We hover in no-man's-land, and nothing gets done.

Abraham left us with a powerful antidote to indecision—faith. He steadfastly believed God's promise to take him to a new land to start a new people. Without hesitation, Abraham obeyed. He left his country, his friends, his family, and everything that was familiar to him and started out one step at a time. He never looked back, but got stronger with every step he took, until he reached the Promised Land where the Jews live today. Then he built an altar to God and gave Him all the glory. What if Abraham had never taken that first step?

Where do you need to stop wavering and take the first step of faith?

PRAYER

Lord Jesus, help me not to waver in my faith but to trust You completely and be strengthened in the process.

CLIMB HIGHER

*We who are **strong** ought to*
bear with the failings of the weak
and not to please ourselves.
Romans 15:1

B ecoming a Christian is just the first rung on the ladder of faith. We can choose to be satisfied that we are saved and stay on the first rung or we can look up and want to go higher and higher in our relationship with Jesus. The higher we go, the more knowledge and understanding we acquire, and the more capable we become to help someone else go higher in their faith. Every new believer needs a stronger believer to encourage them.

Looking back over my life, I am thankful for the mature believers God put in my path who patiently encouraged me and loved me where I was. They made me want to be like them. They encouraged me to climb higher.

Where are you on the ladder of faith and where do you want to be?

PRAYER

Lord Jesus, help me want to climb higher in my faith so I am equipped to help someone else climb higher in theirs.

STAND STRONG

Be on your guard; stand firm in the faith;
be men of courage; be **strong.**
1 Corinthians 16:13

Believers will always face opposition, because unbelievers feel threatened by our beliefs. There is no viable argument against God, against His Word, and against His Son—and what He did for us on the cross—that can stand against His truth. Paul faced such opposition in his day, and we continue to face it in ours.

If our faith is making a difference in our lives and people see it, we will experience opposition. Our response should be to expect it, prepare for it, and then stand strong against it. If we don't stand strong in our faith and commitment to Jesus Christ, we will fall for anything. Don't back down. Don't fall to the enemy. Be courageous and stand strong.

What opposition are you experiencing right now because of your faith? How are you dealing with it?

PRAYER

Lord Jesus, help me stand strong in my faith, so others will see my strength comes from You.

DELIGHT IN YOUR WEAKNESS

*That is why, for Christ's sake, I delight in weaknesses,
in insults, in hardships, in persecutions, in difficulties.
For when I am weak, then I am **strong.***
2 Corinthians 12:10

P aul's thinking in this verse is counter intuitive to our way of thinking. Why would we ever delight in insults or hardships or persecutions or difficulties? We tend to think there is something wrong with people who do. And yet those are the things that draw us closer to Christ, because they are beyond our ability to fix or control.

The fact is we need Jesus, because we will never skate through life problem free. We only experience His strength when we have none left of our own. That's when, for His sake, we delight in being weak.

Where are you feeling weak right now and need Jesus' strength?

PRAYER

Lord Jesus, help me be like Paul and delight in being weak, so You can be my strength.

GET FIT NOW

---

*Finally, be **strong** in the Lord*
and in his mighty power.
Ephesians 6:10

We become strong physically by working out and lifting weights. We become strong spiritually by living in obedience to God's Word. His Word holds us accountable to living life His way instead of our way, and strengthens us so we can.

As believers, we cannot separate ourselves from the Word of God, nor can we change it or ignore part of it to suit our preferences. The entire Bible is centered on Jesus and leads us to Him, so we can experience His power working in our lives now and be fit to live in His Kingdom forever. There is no shortcut and no other way to becoming spiritually fit than reading and obeying God's Word. Time to get fit!

Do you need to rev up your spiritual fitness program by spending time in God's Word?

PRAYER

Lord Jesus, help me diligently study Your Word, so I am spiritually fit.

June 25

BE STRONG IN JESUS

*I can do everything through
him who gives me **strength**.*
Philippians 4:13

Leading sports manufacturers use different slogans and logos to motivate their customers to buy their products and make them feel strong in their physical pursuits. The slogans and logos adorn sweat suits and t-shirts to make people feel like they belong to a special club of sports enthusiasts.

Believers belong to a special club of spiritual enthusiasts. With Jesus as our Coach, there is nothing we cannot do that He has planned for us to do, because we have His strength to draw on. So even when we think we can't go any further, He is always there, cheering us on. He is our biggest fan, and He gives us the strength. So let go of your doubts and be strong in Jesus!

What is God calling you to do that you don't have the strength to do?

PRAYER

Lord Jesus, please remove my doubts and give me Your strength to do what You have called me to do.

June 26

THE TRIP OF A LIFETIME

*May he **strengthen** your hearts
so that you will be blameless and holy
in the presence of our God and
Father when our Lord Jesus comes
with all his holy ones.*
1 Thessalonians 3:13

Do you have a special trip on your bucket list that you would like to take before you die? Do you have it all planned out in your mind? Do you know exactly what you have to do to make it happen?

Jesus has the trip of a lifetime planned for all believers, and He has given us everything we need to make it happen. He has given us Himself, so we can be blameless and holy before His Father in Heaven, and He has given us His Word to strengthen us until we get there. He has prepared us well for the trip. It's all planned. It's on His calendar. The date is set. We will come with Him and all the believers who have gone before us, when He returns to establish His kingdom here on earth (Rev 19:14). Talk about the trip of a lifetime!

How is His Word giving you strength every day until that day comes?

PRAYER

Lord Jesus, help me be strengthened by Your Word every day so I am ready for the trip of a lifetime.

FINISH STRONG

*May our Lord Jesus Christ himself and God our Father . . . encourage your hearts and **strengthen** you in every good deed and word.*
2 Thessalonians 2:16-17

Are you tired of always being the person who says "yes" and not being appreciated? Are you tired of always being there for others, but others not always being there for you? Are you tired of always being the peace maker in your family? Are you tired of being called "the good Christian," because you follow Jesus and try to obey His Word? Are you tired of being taken for granted?

So was a missionary couple returning to the States after many years in another country sharing the gospel. They were exhausted, broke, and discouraged. So they did what they always did, they prayed. And God told them not to worry, they weren't home yet. This assurance gave them the strength to keep going and finish strong. He will do the same for you.

Are you discouraged today? Will you ask God to encourage you?

PRAYER

Lord Jesus, You know I am discouraged. Please encourage me like only You can, so I can finish strong.

June 28

WALK WITH HIM

*But the Lord stood at my side and gave me **strength**.*
2 Timothy 4:17

What do you do when you are feeling weary and exhausted? Go for a run, a hike, a swim, play tennis, listen to your favorite music, or read a book? All good things for sure, but merely a temporary fix.

Only Jesus can breathe into us new energy, new focus, and new strength that will sustain us, because He is the Living God. His resources never run dry. The benefits of the run, the hike, the swim, and the game never end with Him by our side. The music keeps playing and His Book is inexhaustible. He walks with us through life to make sure we make it to the finish line, not just somehow, but triumphantly. Be sure you are walking with Him.

Are you following Jesus at an arms distance or letting Him walk beside you?

PRAYER

Lord Jesus, thank You for being my constant companion. Help me stay close to You.

TRADE IT IN

*Weakness was turned to **strength**.*
Hebrews 11:34

Hebrews 11 records a long list of people in the Old Testament who believed God and trusted His promises. From Abel, who offered God a proper sacrifice because of his faith, to the prophets who conquered kingdoms, administered justice, shut the mouths of lions, quenched fiery flames, and escaped the edge of the sword because of their faith. Their human weakness was turned into supernatural strength and ours can be too.

There is no need to cower in fear or be afraid of what's going to happen tomorrow, because Jesus has given us His strength to live in this world until He comes. Time to trade in our fear for His strength.

Where do you need God's supernatural strength today?

PRAYER

Lord Jesus, please replace my weakness with Your strength, so I can be effective for You until You return.

WAKE UP!

Wake up! **Strengthen** *what remains
and is about to die, for I have not found your
deeds complete in the sight of my God.*
Revelation 3:2

N o one likes to be jolted out of a sound sleep by an
annoying alarm clock. But it's a necessary annoy-
ance if we want to be on time. God is sounding the alarm
to the church in Sardis, because they had fallen asleep in
their faith. The materialism around them had seduced them
away from Him. They were going through the motions, but
their hearts were far from Him, and they refused to repent
and turn back.

Could it be that God is sounding the same alarm today?
Could it be that too many Christians are talking the talk but
not walking the walk? They blend in with the world, instead
of standing out in the world. I hear the alarm. It's time for
the Church to wake up!

Are you an active member of a church that is alive, or does
it need a wake-up call?

PRAYER

Lord Jesus, help me and the other members of my church
be active and discerning, so that our church stays awake.

July

JOY

Be filled with **joy** on your journey of faith.

SHOUT FOR JOY

*Fire came down from the presence of the Lord and consumed the burnt offering and the fat portions on the altar. And when all the people saw it, they shouted for **joy** and fell facedown.*
Leviticus 9:24

Joy is not just being happy when something good happens to us. Joy wells up from deep within us when we are right with God. Moses and Aaron had just offered a sacrifice to God on behalf of the Israelites and God was pleased. His glory appeared to them and fire consumed their offering. This should have terrified them, but it did the opposite—it filled them with joy. They shouted out their praises and fell to the ground to worship Him.

There is simply nothing better than knowing God is pleased with us. We can be going through the worst of circumstances, but that cannot rob us of our joy when we are right with Him. As we continue our journey of faith, let's be right with God and shout for joy.

Are you filled with joy because you know you are right with God?

PRAYER

Lord Jesus, I want to be filled with Your joy, show me where I need to be right with You so I am.

BE COMPLETE

For the Lord your God will bless you . . .
in all the work of your hands,
*and your **joy** will be complete.*
Deuteronomy 16:15

God blessed the Israelites when they gathered to worship Him exactly the way He told them to. He was training them to understand that obedience and worship go hand in hand. They could not worship Him any way they wanted to, and neither can we.

God rightly demands and deserves our utmost attention and devotion. But unfortunately, our worship can be so casual, flippant, and forced, that we not only mock His holiness and miss His blessing, but we also miss the joy. We need to learn this lesson from the Israelites. True worship fills us with joy and makes us complete. Be complete!

Does your worship of God fill you with joy and make you feel complete?

PRAYER

Lord Jesus, please help me worship You with my utmost attention and devotion, so I am filled with joy and feel complete.

CELEBRATE

Splendor and majesty are before him;
*strength and **joy** in his dwelling place.*
1 Chronicles 16:27

We can't imagine God's splendor and majesty. But we do have creation to help us. Think about the most spectacular sunrise and sunset you've ever seen— bookends to our days that are filled with amazing beauty, from delicate flowers to majestic mountains, from sparkling waters to towering trees.

The psalmist had it right when he said the heavens declare the glory of God (Psalm 19:1). And Isaiah brings it down to earth when he says all of creation is the work of His hands (Isaiah 40:28). It only stands to reason that God is the source of our strength and joy. When we look beyond our troubled world and think about His splendor and majesty, we have both. We have much to celebrate.

When is the last time you celebrated the majesty of God?

PRAYER

Lord Jesus, help me pause to celebrate Your majesty so I experience Your strength and joy in my life.

July 4

STAND FOR FREEDOM

*There was great **joy** in Jerusalem,*
for since the days of Solomon son of David King of
Israel there had been nothing like this in Jerusalem.
2 Chronicles 30:26

King Hezekiah sent word to all of Israel and Judah telling the Jews to return to Jerusalem to celebrate the Passover as the people of God. They destroyed the idols that had been set up by previous kings and recommitted themselves to Him. Their joy was so great, they continued their celebration for fourteen days.

Today is the day we celebrate the birthday of our country. We were founded as a nation under God and we need to recommit ourselves to Him. We need to destroy the idols that threaten to replace Him. We need to fight to keep Him in our schools, on our bills, and in our Pledge of Allegiance. We need to stand for our freedoms because we will never have joy if we don't.

What can you do to help reclaim our nation for God?

PRAYER

Lord Jesus, show me what I can do to help reclaim our country for You so we continue to enjoy the freedoms You have given us.

BE FILLED WITH JOY

*Do not grieve, for the **joy**
of the Lord is your strength.*
Nehemiah 8:10

The Jews returned to Jerusalem after being held captive in Babylon for seventy years. Nehemiah, the governor, gathered the people together in the town square, and Ezra, the priest, read from the Law of Moses. As Ezra read and taught the people, they were overcome with emotion and wept. They bowed, with their faces to the ground, and worshiped God. Nehemiah declared the day sacred. Their joy in the Lord overcame their grief and gave them strength.

What would happen in our country if we put our differences aside and came together as one to worship God? He would fill us with joy and renew our strength!

Whom can you invite to worship God and study His Word with you?

PRAYER

Lord Jesus, show me whom I can invite to worship and study Your Word with me this week.

July 6

GREAT JOY

*And on that day they offered
great sacrifices, rejoicing because
God had given them great **joy**.*
Nehemiah 12:43

God's Spirit fills us with joy when we are staying close to Him. His joy lightens our load and quickens our step. His joy motivates us to forget about ourselves and think about those we can help in His name. His joy causes us to rejoice because we are living in His orbit instead of our own. His joy changes our perspective, our attitude, our purpose, and our direction. His joy helps us look beyond our present troubles and find contentment where we are. His joy comes from deep within us and we can't help but rejoice, because it is greater than anything else.

How are you experiencing God's joy in your life today?

PRAYER

Lord Jesus, help me live for You instead of myself and fill me with great joy.

ETERNAL JOY

*Then I would still have this consolation—
my **joy** in unrelenting pain—that I had not
denied the words of the Holy One.*
Job 6:10

People often wonder why there is so much suffering in the world, and if there is a God, why He allows it. Job's friends were wondering the same thing when they saw him lose everything he had—his wealth, his family, and finally his health. He had gone from the pinnacle of success and happiness, to the depths of hopelessness and despair. Even his friends turned on him.

But in the midst of such loss, Job looked forward to his life after death and consoled himself with the fact that through it all, he had stayed true to God, and that would bring him eternal joy. There will always be suffering in this sin-filled world, but this life is short, and eternity is forever! Let's focus on the forever!

What can you learn from Job's reaction to suffering to help you in your own?

PRAYER

Lord Jesus, help me understand that any suffering I experience here pales in comparison to the joy I will experience in Your presence.

❧

PURE JOY

*He will fill your mouth with laughter
and your lips with shouts of **joy**.
Job 8:21*

Job's faithfulness to God during his time of suffering is a powerful lesson for us. It proves we can never out give God. He is always there to bless our patience, obedience, and trust in Him during difficult times, and we come through it with more than we had before. Most of all, we have a deep sense of satisfaction that we have blessed Him. Our relationship with Him is stronger and we can't help but laugh with pure joy.

Job had everything taken from him except his faith. God knew Job's faith was strong enough to sustain him, so He blessed his later years with more than he had before. Instead of dying old and bitter, Job died with a smile on his face. That's pure joy!

How will you use your suffering to bless God so He can bless you more?

PRAYER

Lord Jesus, help me see my suffering as an opportunity to bless You and experience more of You than I did before.

HAVE IT NOW

He prays to God and finds favor with him,
*he sees God's face and shouts for **joy**;*
he is restored by God to his righteous state.
Job 33:26

P rayer is our lifeline to God. Prayer puts our life in perspective and reminds us that He is in control. Prayer gives us peace in the midst of our doubts, confusion, and stress. Prayer takes the responsibility off us and puts it on God. Prayer pleases God because we are trusting Him to help us.

Job found favor with God because he never stopped praying. We have to wait until we get to Heaven to actually see God, but knowing we have His favor is the next best thing. Grab your lifeline and hold on. He hears, He answers, He restores. And we can have that now.

Do you pray until you sense God's favor with you which always translates as peace?

PRAYER

Lord Jesus, help me to pray fervently so my prayers please You and bring me peace.

July 10

A HEART FULL OF JOY

*You have filled my heart
with greater **joy** than when their
grain and new wine abound.*
Psalm 4:7

D avid knew what we all need to know—that all the material blessings in the world don't compare to the joy that God gives us when we stay close to Him. David was just a teenager when God called him to be king of Israel. At that time, he had no material possessions except perhaps the slingshot he killed Goliath with. We could say he went from rags to riches very quickly.

Even though God knew David would fall into great sin, He also knew his heart would always turn back to Him. God knew He would always be David's greatest joy. With all the material blessings that compete for our attention and affection, what could be better than a heart full of joy?

Does God know He is your greatest joy?

PRAYER

Lord Jesus, help me keep my focus on You so You are always my greatest joy.

JOY RESTORED

*Restore to me the **joy** of your salvation
and grant me a willing spirit, to sustain me.*
Psalm 51:12

David abused his power as king and committed adultery with Bathsheba. One sin led to another, then another. When he found out she was pregnant, David schemed to make it look like her husband, Uriah, was the father. His scheme failed, so he had Uriah put on the front line of battle in the hopes he would be killed, and he was. David was thrown into a cycle of denial, cover-up, hypocrisy, and severe depression.

Sin of any nature does that, because we are disconnecting ourselves from God. Sin robs our joy. The only way back is to do what David did—confess our sin and yield our spirit to Him. God restored David's joy and He will restore ours.

What sin do you need to confess so God can restore your joy?

PRAYER

Lord Jesus, give me a willing spirit to recognize and confess my sin so I am right with You and my joy is restored.

SHOUT IT OUT

*Shout with **joy** to God, all the earth!*
Sing the glories of his name;
make his praise glorious.
Psalm 66:1-2

What would happen if people from every nation on earth stopped what they were doing and gave a huge SHOUT-OUT to God? We could sing our favorite hymns in every language and praise Him for all His blessings. It would be seen all over the world on Facebook and Instagram. It would be the "Breaking News" of the day. It would stop all the fake news, because it's the real news.

God is worthy of our praise. He created this earth for us and us for this earth. He deserves our praise. Unfortunately, we will have to wait until we get to Heaven to hear the nations praise Him, but we can do our part now. Just go outside, look up and shout it out! He will love it.

How often do you shout out your praises to God?

PRAYER

Lord Jesus, You are worthy of my praise. Don't let me go a day without praising You.

July 13

RECLAIM YOUR JOY

Your statutes are my heritage forever;
*they are the **joy** of my heart.*
Psalm 119:111

We live in a world with an "anything goes" mentality. There is no respect for authority and no moral absolutes. People make up their own truth and their own rules. God has been cast aside. His Book has been closed. Consequently, our kids and grandkids are growing up with a false heritage. Most don't even know the Ten Commandments, let alone keep them.

But God will never be mocked or replaced. He has overseen the fall of countless nations because they mocked Him or replaced Him, and they no longer stand. In fact, instead of us scoffing Him, He scoffs at nations who think they can survive without Him (Psalm 2:4). It's time to turn back to God and reclaim our heritage and our joy.

How are you passing down your heritage of faith to your family?

PRAYER

Lord Jesus, help me make it a priority to pass my heritage of faith down to the next generation.

July 14

ENDLESS JOY

---

*The prospect of the righteous is **joy**,*
but the hopes of the wicked come to nothing.
Proverbs 10:28

I t is hard to find joy in our world today. Our country is divided. The crime rate is sky-rocketing. Lawlessness invades our cities. People think nothing of destroying historical monuments. Our national heritage is on the verge of collapse. The evil intent to take good people down is palpable.

But believers have joy, because we know the end of the story. Evil will never overcome good, because Satan will never defeat God. Satan was defeated on the cross, when Jesus died for the sins of the world and made it possible for us to be righteous in God's sight. The wicked may have their heyday now, but the joy of the righteous will continue forever. Our joy will be endless!

How are you allowing your joy to make a difference in the world?

PRAYER

Lord Jesus, help my joy in You be a light in this dark world.

✍

GOODBYE SORROW, HELLO JOY

*Gladness and **joy** will overtake them,
and sorrow and sighing will flee away.*
Isaiah 35:10

While in captivity in Babylon for seventy years, the Israelites were deprived of their land, their worship, their traditions, and their joy. But God gave them this message of hope. Their time of punishment for their disobedience was limited. Their time of being held hostage in a foreign land with a foreign culture and foreign gods would end. Their time of sorrow and grief for all they had lost would pass. They would return to Israel with gladness and joy.

God wants us to know that our times of sorrow are limited as well, and gladness and joy are right around the corner.

Are you in a period of sorrow and grief right now because of a past failure? Give it to Jesus and let Him replace it with gladness and joy.

PRAYER

Lord Jesus, please forgive my sins and replace my sorrow and grief with Your gladness and joy.

July 16

WELCOME HOME

The ransomed of the Lord will return.
They will enter Zion with singing; everlasting
joy *will crown their heads.*
Isaiah 51:11

After their years of captivity were over, Isaiah's prophecy for the Israelites came true. They returned to their own land, and all they had been through became a fleeting memory. They looked forward to being back home in their own country and their own beloved city of Jerusalem.

We can apply this verse to our going home to Heaven after our life here on earth is over. Those who have been ransomed by the Lord, because we have put our faith and trust in Jesus Christ, will be greeted with a huge "Welcome Home!" We won't be able to stop singing or contain our joy. We will wear it as a crown on our heads.

Do people see the joy of the Lord in you?

PRAYER

Lord Jesus, help my joy in You overflow to others so they want to know You too.

July 17

TIME TO WAKE UP

*You will go out in **joy** and be led forth in peace; the mountains and hills will burst forth into song before you, and all the trees of the field will clap their hands.*
Isaiah 55:12

The Israelites left Babylon in joy, because they had learned their lesson. God was their God, and they were His people. Even nature was rejoicing as they returned to their own nation to worship Him.

I wonder what it will take for our nation to remember that we were founded on Christian principles and values. God's Word directed our Founding Fathers, and the Bible was unashamedly read and obeyed in homes, churches, schools, and universities. Not so today. We have lost our way, just as the Israelites did before God allowed them to be taken captive by a foreign power. Time to wake up, America!

Are you aware of the danger our country is in because we have turned our back on God?

PRAYER

Lord Jesus, help this country wake up and find our way back to You, and help me be faithful to pray.

KNOW YOUR PURPOSE

As soon as the sound of your
greeting reached my ears, the baby
in my womb leaped for **joy**.
Luke 1:44

Can you imagine the young Mary going to Elizabeth's house and being greeted with this confirmation of her own destiny as the mother of the coming Messiah? And why wouldn't the unborn John the Baptist leap for joy in his mother's womb on this first encounter with his own Savior? John was honored and thrilled to be Jesus' herald, to be the one to announce to the world, "Behold, the lamb of God who takes away the sin of the world" (John 1:29).

John played a vital role in Jesus' earthly ministry. He knew his purpose and glorified God by fulfilling it. Jesus gives every believer a purpose, and He equips us to fulfill it. Nothing gives Him more glory or us greater joy than doing what He created us to do.

If you don't know God's purpose for you, will you ask Him to show you?

PRAYER

Lord Jesus, show me Your purpose for me so I don't miss the joy, and You don't miss the glory.

JOY TO THE WORLD

*But the angel said to them, "Do not be afraid. I bring you good news of great **joy** that will be for all the people. Today in the town of David a Savior has been born to you; he is Christ the Lord."*
Luke 2:10-11

The Christmas Story thrills us with joy, even in July, because its message is always relevant and timely. God Himself came into this world as one of us. He came as a tiny, helpless baby just like we do. The first people to hear the news were not kings, queens, or presidents, but lowly shepherds tending their sheep.

How appropriate for the Savior of the world, who would call Himself the Good Shepherd who protects His sheep and knows them by name, to identify with these shepherds. They also knew their sheep by name and were always ready to rescue them from harm. No wonder the angel told them not to be afraid. Jesus is the greatest news the world has ever heard. Joy to the World!

How will you celebrate Jesus in your life today?

PRAYER

Lord Jesus, help me celebrate You every day, because You bring joy into this joyless world.

COMPLETE JOY

I have told you this so that my
joy *may be in you and that*
your joy may be complete.
John 15:11

I t was the night of Jesus' Last Supper. He had already told the disciples He was going to die. Now He told them one of them would betray Him, and Peter would deny Him— all bad news He didn't want to leave them with. So Jesus promised He was going to prepare a place for them so they, and all believers after Him, could be with Him where He was going (John 14:3).

Jesus' words have comforted and sustained believers ever since, because nothing we go through on this earth can rob us of the joy it gives us to know we will be with Him. And our joy will be complete when we are.

Are you prepared to comfort others with this great promise?

PRAYER

Lord Jesus, please show me whom I can share this promise with, so their joy can be complete.

FROM GRIEF TO JOY

*I tell you the truth, you will weep and
mourn while the world rejoices. You will grieve,
but your grief will turn to **joy**.*
John 16:20

Jesus was preparing His disciples for when He would be gone. He knew the depth of their sorrow when they would watch Him arrested and led away to die the most brutal death in history. He knew they would doubt everything He had told them about rising again on the third day. And He knew fear for their own fate would drive them into hiding.

So on their way into Gethsemane, Jesus told the disciples what we know to be true—the world rejoiced at His death because people didn't want to hear His message. But the disciples' grief turned to joy, because they got to share His message with the world. Jesus turned their grief to joy, and He does the same for us.

What grief in your life can you give to Jesus, so He can give you His joy?

PRAYER

Lord Jesus, help me give You my grief, so I can receive Your joy.

PASS IT ON

*Out of the most severe trial, their overflowing **joy** and
their extreme poverty welled up in rich generosity.*
2 Corinthians 8:2

The early Christians turned the world upside down. They suffered persecution and even death for their faith in Jesus Christ. Nothing was more important to them than sharing the good news of salvation through Him with anyone and everyone. Even their possessions took second place to their devotion to Him, so they gladly shared what little they had with people who needed it more. Their entire perspective on life and death, meaning and purpose changed. They overflowed with the joy that only comes from Jesus, and everyone they met became the beneficiaries, including us today. Now we have the privilege of passing it on.

Does your love for Jesus express itself in joy and generosity to others?

PRAYER

Lord Jesus, help me follow the example of these early believers so my love for You overflows with joy and generosity.

July 23

WHAT'S YOUR PASSION?

*Then make my **joy** complete by being like-minded,
having the same love, being one in spirit and purpose.*
Philippians 2:2

C an you remember a teacher who inspired you and motivated you to learn, because they were so passionate about what they were teaching? Paul was so passionate about Jesus that he spent his life preaching the gospel, because he wanted everyone to know the difference He had made in his life and could make in theirs. It filled him with joy when people came to faith.

Paul is encouraging believers of every generation to grow in our faith by becoming more and more like Jesus—to think like Him, love like Him, and fulfill our purpose in Him. This was Paul's passion that completed his joy, and it's the passion that will complete ours.

Are you passionate enough about Jesus to want to be more like Him?

PRAYER

Lord Jesus, complete my joy by making me passionate for You.

July 24

JOY IN A JOYLESS WORLD

Therefore, my brothers, you whom
*I love and long for, my **joy** and crown, that is*
how you should stand firm in the Lord, dear friends!
Philippians 4:1

It's hard to stand firm today. Our world feels shaky and insecure. Everything we value as believers is being undermined and threatened. We face the same enemies believers faced two thousand years ago—people who oppose God and stop at nothing to eliminate Him.

Our culture also wants to eliminate Jesus and the Bible, so we must stand firm. We can only stand firm when we remember that Christ in us is greater than any enemy we will ever face, and He is coming again as the final proof. This is the hope of every believer. This is what motivates us to stand firm in a world that has gone off course and lost its way. This is what gives us joy in a joyless world.

Are you allowing the troubles of our times rob you of your joy in Christ?

PRAYER

Lord Jesus, help me stand firm with other believers in the sheer joy of knowing You are in control and coming back to make things right.

THE GREAT REUNION

*For what is our hope, our **joy**, or the crown
in which we glory in the presence of our Lord
Jesus when he comes? Is it not you? Indeed,
you are our glory and **joy**.*
1 Thessalonians 2:19-20

One of the greatest joys we will experience in Heaven is seeing the people we shared Jesus with so they could be there too. This is what Paul lived for, and it should be what we live for, because at the end of the day and the end of our life, nothing else matters. Nothing is more important than sharing our faith, because nothing else will follow us from this life into the next.

Watching my husband of fifty-six years soften his heart and surrender to Jesus in the last years of his life is one of my greatest joys, because I know with absolute certainty that he is in His presence now, and I am looking forward to the great reunion we will have someday.

Whom are you looking forward to seeing in Heaven because you shared Jesus with them?

PRAYER

Lord Jesus, help me be ready and willing to share You with the people who cross my path today.

REFRESH YOUR JOY

*Your love has given me great **joy** and*
encouragement, because you, brother,
have refreshed the hearts of the saints.
Philemon 7

We all need to be encouraged in our faith. We need each other. That's why Christ started the Church. But today, we are in the middle of a global pandemic and our churches are closed. Fortunately, that has not stopped believers from encouraging one another.

We can text, email, Facetime, Instagram, livestream, Zoom, Skype, and watch YouTube videos. We can join worship services all over the world, day or night. So even though we may be in lockdown or quarantine, God has provided a time like never before for believers to stay connected and be encouraged, because the future of the Church depends on it. So, let's love each other and refresh our joy.

How can you reach out to someone to encourage them in their faith, so their joy is refreshed and yours is too?

PRAYER

Lord Jesus, in difficult times show me how I can connect with other believers, so we can love and encourage each other.

July 27

LOOKING TOWARD HOME

*Let us fix our eyes on Jesus, the author and perfecter
of our faith, who for the **joy** set before him endured
the cross, scorning its shame, and sat down at the
right hand of the throne of God.*
Hebrews 12:2

How could this be? How could Jesus approach the cross with joy when He knew the brutality and pain that awaited Him, and the shame of bearing our sin when He had no sin of His own? We cannot fathom such love, such resolve, such determination, such commitment, such obedience. But that's exactly what motivated Him.

In the Garden of Gethsemane, Jesus looked beyond the agony of the cross to what it would mean for you and for me. And He thought about being back Home sitting at His Father's right hand and all of us being with Him. That's how Jesus approached the cross. Let us fix our eyes on Him, and for the joy set before us endure what we are facing, because we have Home to look forward to also.

What hard thing are you anticipating right now that you can trust Jesus to see you through?

PRAYER

Lord Jesus, help me fix my eyes on You and trust You to see me through—with joy.

CONSIDER IT JOY

*Consider it pure **joy**, my brothers, whenever you face trials of many kinds . . . so that you may be mature and complete, not lacking anything.*
James 1:2-4

Trials move us forward in our journey of faith faster than anything else, because they push us out of our comfort zone. We are forced to depend on God instead of ourselves and our own resources. Circumstances and timing are out of our control, so we have to depend on God. Our faith matures in the process, because we develop patience and perseverance.

James says, change your attitude about the trials you are going through. Look at them differently. They are not a bad thing. They are actually a good thing, because they draw you closer to God. And as you mature in your faith, you will realize you have everything you need, most of all, joy.

Will you ask God to help you change your attitude toward the trials you face?

PRAYER

Lord Jesus, help me see my trials as opportunities to trust You more and mature in my faith.

July 29

INEXPRESSIBLE AND GLORIOUS JOY

Though you have not seen him, you love him;
and even though you do not see him now,
you believe in him and are filled with an
inexpressible and glorious **joy.**
1 Peter 1:8

Peter was called by Jesus, worked with Jesus, prayed with Jesus, cried with Jesus, and was the first to confess Jesus as the Christ, the Son of the Living God (Matthew 16:16). Jesus told him he was blessed by those firsthand experiences that helped him believe. But many more would follow who would not see, touch, or hear Him, and believe anyway.

Perhaps Peter was recalling his conversation with Jesus when he confessed his faith. And he wrote these words to encourage all of us who love Jesus and believe in Him, even though we do not see Him. But the result is the same—inexpressible and glorious joy!

What is your joy level because you love and follow Jesus?

PRAYER

Lord Jesus, increase my joy in You and let it spill over to everyone I meet.

July 30

ꙮ

TEACH THE TRUTH

---

*It has given me great **joy** to find some of your children walking in the truth, just as the Father commanded us.*
2 John 4

I received the legacy of faith in Jesus Christ from my maternal grandmother. As a mother, grandmother, and great grandmother, nothing gives me more joy than knowing this legacy is being passed down to the next generation, and the next after that. I loved my four-year-old great grandson's prayer for the Covid-19 pandemic. He said, "Dear God, I know You can fix it because You have all the power. Amen."

We know God loves the faith of little children—so confident, blunt, and honest. No wonder He commands us to teach them the truth of the gospel. Then as they become adults, it is up to them to manage their walk, and up to us to pray they will.

Are you teaching your children the truth of the gospel, so they can pass it on to theirs?

PRAYER

Lord Jesus, help me teach my children the truth of the gospel, so it will pass on to the generations that follow.

A PARENT'S JOY

*I have no greater **joy** than to hear
that my children are walking in the truth.*
3 John 4

When my oldest granddaughter, who has two of my great grandchildren, saw this verse fell on her birthday she said, "That's perfect. I can't imagine anything better!" What parent wouldn't agree? We pray and plead, we laugh and cry, we teach and preach, we love and forgive, and we hope, as our children grow up and move on with their lives. This world can easily lead them away from the truth.

But there is only one truth, and His name is Jesus. So we pray our children will study the Bible and walk with Him, because we know He will show them the way and lead them safely Home. And our lives will be blessed with the greatest joy a parent can experience until we are with them again.

How often do you pray for your children and their families to walk in the truth?

PRAYER

Lord Jesus, help me be diligent in praying for my children and their families so they walk with You.

August

GRACE

Thank God for His **grace**
on your journey of faith.

WEAR GRACE

*Listen, my son, to your father's instruction and do not forsake your mother's teaching. They will be a garland to **grace** your head and a chain to adorn your neck.*
Proverbs 1:8-9

Grace is a beautiful word with many wonderful meanings—beauty, charm, decency, thoughtfulness, good will, favor, blessing. All are embodied in God's definition of grace: His unmerited love and favor toward us. Whether we grew up in a home where this truth was taught or not, we've probably all heard the familiar hymn, "Amazing Grace," written by John Newton. The first verse says it all: "Amazing Grace! How sweet the sound that saved a wretch like me! I once was lost but now am found; was blind, but now I see."

Salvation is God's grace to us. As we continue our journey of faith, make sure and claim it. Pass it on to your children. Let it adorn your life. Wear grace, and everyone you meet will be blessed.

Have you accepted God's gift of salvation? With whom can you share this wonderful news?

PRAYER

Lord Jesus, thank You for Your grace in my life. Help me wear it proudly and bless others in the process.

GRACE YOUR PRESENCE

My son, preserve sound judgment
and discernment, do not let them out
of your sight; they will be life for you,
*an ornament to **grace** your neck.*
Proverbs 3:21-22

We live in a world that needs sound judgment and discernment like never before. Our world is upside down in chaos, corruption, and confusion. A thousand voices vie for our attention and confound our thinking.

God's Word is our only source of truth and wisdom, and therefore, the only way we can have His judgment and discernment. We must drown out the other voices and listen to His. We must know His Word and live it out in our lives in the way we think, speak, and act. God's Word is the life this world needs. Let's be sure His Word graces your presence and mine.

To whom or what do you turn for sound judgment and discernment other than God?

PRAYER

Lord Jesus, You are the source of sound judgment and discernment. Help me drown out the other voices and listen and obey Yours.

August 3

KNOW YOUR PLACE

*He mocks proud mockers
but gives **grace** to the humble.*
Proverbs 3:34

God's grace and human pride are incompatible. They are like oil and water—they don't mix. God will simply not compete with us. Either we let Him be God, or we remain our own god. But if we choose that path, we need to be aware of the danger.

God will always be God regardless of our opinion of Him. And God will always be sovereign over us whether we think He is or not. So it's best to be on His side, because He will give us what we deserve if we oppose Him, but He will give us what we don't deserve if we honor and serve Him. God laughs at the foolishness of the proud and extends His grace to those who know their place before Him. It is critical we know our place.

How do you let your pride get in the way of God's grace in your life?

PRAYER

Lord Jesus, help me humble myself before You and accept Your grace.

August 4

GRACE POURED OUT

*And I will pour out on the house of David
and the inhabitants of Jerusalem a spirit
of **grace** and supplication.*
Zechariah 12:10

Where would we be without God's grace poured out on the nation of Israel? We would be without the Son of God, the Word of God, and the people of God. In His sovereignty, God chose Israel to be His nation and her people to be His people through whom He would send the Savior into the world.

The Israelites rejected Jesus as their Savior, but Israel is still God's nation, and her people are still His people. God kept His promise the first time and Jesus came, and He will fulfill this promise when Jesus returns. God's grace will be poured out once more, and the Jewish people will finally recognize Jesus as their own. Jesus is God's grace poured out!

How do you show your appreciation and gratitude for the nation of Israel and her people?

PRAYER

Lord Jesus, help me love, appreciate, and pray for Your nation of Israel and her people.

LIVE FOR HIM

*And the child grew and became strong; he was filled with wisdom, and the **grace** of God was upon him.*
Luke 2:40

Can you imagine living in the same household with Jesus? Can you imagine being Mary, Joseph, or His siblings and never hearing Jesus talk back or use bad language; never seeing Him bully His friends or show lack of respect for His parents; never being critical, judgmental, or mean; never lying, stealing, or cheating on an exam; never doing ANYTHING wrong; but always being the One everyone wanted to be with.

Jesus knew God loved Him and He knew His identity was with Him. He grew in that relationship and became strong physically, mentally, emotionally, and spiritually. He grew in wisdom and grace. Jesus lived for us, so we can live for Him.

Are you living your life for Jesus?

PRAYER

Lord Jesus, please help me grow in my relationship with You and live my life for You.

August 6

❧

SEE IT AS GRACE

*From the fullness of his **grace** we have
all received one blessing after another.*
John 1:16

We can all look back in our lives and see God's grace on our behalf—blessings we have enjoyed that we did not deserve; blessings we cannot claim to be of our own making; blessings that had His hand all over them.

Once we see these blessings as God's intervention, our relationship with Him changes. We take our proper position before Him as He is our Creator, our Savior, and our God. We are humbled by His intimate love, His tender care, His personal provision, His sustaining strength. And we are blessed some more, because we see it for what it is—grace!

What blessings in your life do you recognize as God's grace to you?

PRAYER

Lord Jesus, help me recognize the blessings in my life as Your grace to me and nothing I did to deserve.

GOD'S PERFECT SOLUTION

*For the law was given
through Moses; **grace** and truth
came through Jesus Christ.
John 1:17*

We are experiencing lawlessness in our cities today that is more reflective of the Wild West in the nineteenth century than our sophistication in the twenty-first century. Lawlessness is the reason God gave the Israelites laws to live by, so they would survive as the nation that would produce Jesus.

Since that time, the Ten Commandments remain as God's timeless law for every generation—to keep us safe and help us survive. We need both the law and order God gave us and the grace and truth Jesus gives us—God's perfect solution for a world behaving more like the Wild West than the sophisticated people He calls us to be.

Do you know and obey God's commandments and, therefore, experience Jesus' grace and truth?

PRAYER

Lord Jesus, help me know and obey Your commandments and be thankful for Your grace and truth in my life.

August 8

☙

DON'T KEEP IT
TO YOURSELF

*With great power the apostles
continued to testify to the resurrection
of the Lord Jesus, and much **grace**
was upon them all.
Acts 4:33*

Death by crucifixion was common in first century Rome. It was reserved for the worst criminals as a deterrent. People were used to seeing this brutal spectacle, so when Jesus died on the cross that Friday, people didn't pay much attention. The disciples didn't have a story to tell or a gospel to preach UNTIL they discovered the empty tomb on Sunday morning. The greatest story ever told needed to be told. And tell it they did. Even their own eventual deaths couldn't stop the news from spreading.

Jesus' resurrection couldn't keep the disciples silent, and it shouldn't keep us silent. Because His tomb is empty, ours will be too. Don't keep this life-giving news to yourself.

Whom can you share this great news with, so their tomb will be empty too?

PRAYER

Lord Jesus, help me speak boldly of Your resurrection to someone who needs to hear it today.

August 9

MAKE IT COUNT

*I consider my life nothing to me,
if only I may finish the race and complete the task the
Lord Jesus has given me—the task of testifying to the
gospel of God's* **grace**.
Acts 20:24

The apostle Paul never got over God's grace in his life. After all, he had Christians murdered before his personal encounter with Jesus on his way to Damascus. In a flash of lightning, Paul's life was changed forever. Jesus changed his direction, his focus, his heart, his attitude, his belief system, and his name.

Paul spent the rest of his life marveling at the grace he had been given and worked tirelessly to share it with whoever would listen. From kings and queens to prison guards. From elite Jews to pagan Gentiles. Paul stopped at nothing, because he knew he would only live once, and he wanted to make it count—for Jesus. We can too. Make your life count!

How is your life making a difference for Jesus?

PRAYER

Lord Jesus, help my life count for You, because in the end nothing else matters.

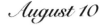

August 10

GO FOR IT!

Through him and for his name's sake, we received **grace** *and apostleship to call people from among all the gentiles to the obedience that comes from faith.*
Romans 1:5

My oldest grandson is heading off to Law School this fall even though classes will be online because of the pandemic. I admire his determination and commitment to follow through with his plans. That is the advantage we have as Christians when we believe God has called us to a certain work. Nothing will deter us from it.

God called Paul to preach the gospel outside of Israel to non-Jews or gentiles—a daunting task—but God equipped him for it. He used Paul's intelligent mind and educational background, together with His grace, to reach people who had never heard of Jesus. God equips us to do what He calls us to do, so go for it!

What seemingly daunting task is God calling you to today?

PRAYER

Lord Jesus, help me trust You to equip me for the work You call me to do.

CALLED TO BE SAINTS

*To all in Rome who are loved by God and called to be saints: **Grace** and peace to you from God our Father and from the Lord Jesus Christ.*
Romans 1:7

God calls us all to be saints. The term is not reserved just for people who pass certain human standards but for all people who come to faith in Jesus Christ. God makes no distinction between nations, races, cultures, languages, religions, or church denominations. The ground is level at the foot of the cross. All are welcome. He loves us all, and He calls us all to Him, because only in Him can He show us His grace and give us His peace.

God strategically placed Paul in Rome, so this message would go out to the whole world and continue down through the generations. Nothing would stop it, because God wants us to come to faith in Jesus Christ. He calls us all to be saints.

Do you see yourself as a saint because you believe in Jesus Christ?

PRAYER

Lord Jesus, thank You for setting me apart for Yourself and calling me a saint. Help me live up to it.

FOUND

*For all have sinned and fall short of the glory of God,
and are justified freely by his **grace** through the
redemption that came by Christ Jesus.*
Romans 3:23-24

My daughter was distraught when she discovered one of the diamond earrings her husband had given her was missing. They looked all over to no avail—until that evening and the lighting was perfect. There it was at the bottom of their pool. The lost had been found.

We lost the glory God intended for us in the Garden of Eden when sin entered the human race. But that glory is found when we come to Christ. Our sins are forgiven. We are justified or declared "not guilty" and made righteous again by God's grace. Jesus has redeemed us. We are found, and our glory is restored before God.

Whom can you pray for to be restored in Christ?

PRAYER

Lord Jesus, help me lead others to You so they are found, and their glory is restored.

JUST GRACE

*And if by **grace**, then it is no longer*
*by works; if it were, **grace** would*
*no longer be **grace**.*
Romans 11:6

W hy is it so hard for us to realize that there is simply nothing we can do to save ourselves or even help God save us from our sinful condition? The answer is—we like to be in control of our own lives. Our pride collides with God's grace. If God's grace alone saves us, nothing else is needed. Otherwise, Jesus' death on the cross was unnecessary. If grace is not grace, it begs the question—how many good works or what kind of works would we have to do to earn our salvation? And what kind of Heaven would it be if we did get there on our own? Thanks be to God for settling the matter for us. We cannot save ourselves. We are saved by grace—just grace.

Do you still struggle with this issue of your works vs. God's grace to save you?

PRAYER

Lord Jesus, help me settle this matter once and for all. There is nothing I can do to save myself. I need Your grace.

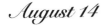

DON'T WASTE THE GIFT

*But by the **grace** of God I am what I am, and his*
***grace** to me was not without effect. No, I worked*
*harder than all of them—yet not I, but the **grace** of*
God that was with me.
1 Corinthians 15:10

Have you ever received a gift, opened it, used it, and then put it away and forgotten it for a while? God's grace can be like that. We can receive it, open it, use it, and then put it away and forget it for a while. But Paul would say, that's a waste! He sets the example of how we should use God's grace. He received it, opened it, used it, and kept on using it. And the more he used it, the more it multiplied.

God's grace is truly the gift that keeps on giving. It becomes ours the moment we receive God's free gift of salvation in Jesus Christ and stays with us the rest of our lives. God's grace makes us who we are and who we are to become. Don't waste the gift of His grace.

How is God's grace blessing your life?

PRAYER

Lord Jesus, thank You for Your grace in my life. Help me grow in my faith because of it.

August 15

DO IT ALL

*But just as you excel in everything—in faith,
in speech, in knowledge, in complete
earnestness and in your love for us—see that
you also exceed in this **grace** of giving.*
2 Corinthians 8:7

The generosity of the early Church was amazing. People were not only willing to speak up for their faith, grow in their faith, and die for their faith, they were also willing to give everything they had to help the Church grow. Paul commended this church in Corinth for their strengths. Now he urged them to take the next step and excel in their giving.

We know what we value by looking at how and where we spend our money. Where our money goes reflects our values. The Church in the first century depended on the generosity of the people, and so does the Church in the twenty-first century. Let's excel in faith, speech, knowledge, love, **and** giving. Let's do it all.

How does your giving and mine reflect our commitment to the Church around the world and our church at home?

PRAYER

Lord Jesus, help me give thoughtfully and generously to Your Church around the world and at home.

BE RICH

*For you know the **grace** of our Lord Jesus Christ,
that though he was rich, yet for your sakes
he became poor, so that you through his
poverty might become rich.*
2 Corinthians 8:9

Grace—God's Riches At Christ's Expense. Jesus became poor so we could become rich. It's hard to imagine Him leaving the glory of Heaven and coming down here to live like one of us. But He did, and we are forever the beneficiaries. Jesus left the presence of His Father, the glory He had as His Son, the beauty and perfection of Paradise, and the company of people like Abraham, Moses, David, Esther, and Ruth—just to name some—because He wanted us to experience all the joys of Heaven with Him. Jesus set His glory and majesty aside and came into our world to a poor family who could only swaddle Him in rags, so we could be rich, really rich.

How rich are you? How much of Jesus do you have in your life?

PRAYER

Lord Jesus, help my life reflect my gratitude for the riches I have in You.

HIS POWER—NOT MINE

*My **grace** is sufficient for you,*
for my power is made perfect in your weakness.
2 Corinthians 12:9

P aul knew what it was to be weak. He had suffered just about every hardship imaginable as he fulfilled Jesus' call to tell the world about Him. But Paul never complained about any of these obstacles except one. Apparently, he had a nagging problem that he asked Jesus to remove three different times and each time the answer was no (2 Corinthians 12:8). We have to wonder why.

Why didn't Jesus want to make Paul's work easier? Why didn't He cure him so he wasn't in constant pain and could do even more? The answer is as much for us as it was for Paul—because when we are weak, we see His power at work, and when we are strong, we see our power at work.

Whose power do you see at work in what you are doing for Jesus, yours or His?

PRAYER

Lord Jesus, help me depend on Your power to accomplish the work You call me to do.

August 18

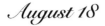

SEND A BLESSING

*May the **grace** of the Lord Jesus Christ,
and the love of God, and the fellowship of
the Holy Spirit be with you all.*
2 Corinthians 13:14

When is the last time you sat down and wrote a letter—a real, honest-to-goodness letter, in your own handwriting on real stationary? Texting and email have become our preferred communication in the twenty-first century. Paul would not like our terse messages and abrupt endings. But we can learn from him and how he ended this letter to the church in Corinth.

Paul evokes the three Persons of the Trinity to bless his readers—the grace of Jesus, the love of the Father, and the fellowship of the Holy Spirit. Who wouldn't like to get a letter like that, or a text or an email? Send a blessing.

Whom can you bless with Paul's benediction today?

PRAYER

Lord Jesus, help me use this benediction to bless someone.

THE RIGHT GOSPEL

*I am astonished that you are
so quickly deserting the one who
called you by the **grace** of Christ and
are turning to a different gospel—which
is really no gospel at all.
Galatians 1:6-7*

There is always the danger of hearing a different gospel than the pure gospel of Jesus Christ. False teaching crept into the early Church, and it remains with us today. But there is only one gospel. And Paul could not believe some of these believers were turning away from God and the grace of His forgiveness through Jesus Christ.

No other religion has a Savior who died for us. No other Savior left His position in Heaven and came down to us, died a brutal death, and then rose from the dead three days later. Any gospel that teaches differently is bad news instead of good news, because it comes from Satan instead of God. Make sure you hear the right gospel.

Are you knowledgeable enough of the gospel to detect when it is not taught?

PRAYER

Lord Jesus, help me know Your gospel so I know when it's not being taught.

August 20

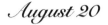

ONE OR THE OTHER
---

*You who are trying to be justified by
law have been alienated from Christ;
you have fallen away from **grace**.*
Galatians 5:4

We can't have it both ways. We can't try to be good enough to earn God's favor and depend on His grace at the same time. Either we are depending on ourselves and our own goodness to get us into His Heaven, or we are depending on His. Either we accept His grace to us in sending Jesus to justify us before God, or we reject it and die in our sins. Our goodness simply will never be good enough.

It's a decision we all must make—keep trying to justify ourselves before a holy and perfect God or accept the free gift of His grace through Jesus Christ. It's the most important decision we will ever make. Where we spend eternity hangs in the balance.

How are you still trying to earn God's favor instead of depending on His grace for your salvation?

PRAYER

Lord Jesus, help me be fully dependent on Your grace through faith in You for my salvation.

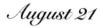

LAVISHED WITH GRACE

In him we have redemption through his blood,
the forgiveness of sins, in accordance with
*the riches of God's **grace** that he lavished on us*
with all wisdom and understanding.
Ephesians 1:7-8

Can you imagine God looking down through the ages of history, knowing how defiant, disobedient, and just plain wicked we would be, and still loving us enough to forgive us? And then coming Himself in human form to be the atoning sacrifice that would pay the debt for our sin and permit us to live with Him forever? What kind of god does that?

Only a God so rich in grace that He can't separate Himself from it. It is who He is. He created us in His image to love Him, and He lavishes us with His grace so we can know Him and love Him in return. Only through His grace can we understand our desperate need for Him. Open your heart wide to receive it.

How are you showing your gratitude to God for His grace in your life?

PRAYER

Lord Jesus, help me show off the riches of Your grace in my life, so others will want it too.

August 22

OPEN THE GIFT
---

*For it is by **grace** you have been saved, through faith—and this not from yourselves, it is the gift of God—not by works, so that no one can boast.*
Ephesians 2:8-9

Picture yourself in Heaven and everyone vying for the opportunity to tell us how they got there. Can you imagine the long lists of personal achievements and successes we would have to listen to, and people competing back and forth for the most noteworthy?

God couldn't either! In fact, nothing would ruin His Heaven more than it being just like here on earth. So He leveled the field with His grace. No one gets in without it. Now picture yourself in Heaven and everyone vying for the opportunity to love Him, thank Him, worship Him, and serve Him. And everyone loving everyone else, because we all got there the same way—we opened the gift of His grace.

Whom can you share this life-changing news with?

PRAYER

Lord Jesus, help me share the gift of Your grace with someone today.

GIVE BACK

*But to each one of us **grace** has
been given as Christ apportioned it.*
Ephesians 4:7

Have you ever looked at your kids and wondered how they could be so different? One might be musical, one might be athletic, one might be super energetic, one might be mellow. And you think, how could the same two parents produce so much variety? The answer is—God loves variety.

God uses variety in our families to make them interesting and useful and to keep us on our knees. He uses variety in His Church to accomplish His purpose in the world. Out of His abundant grace, He gives all believers gifts to use for His glory. Gifts like serving, teaching, encouraging, generosity, hospitality, leadership—gifts to give back to Jesus. It's fun to give back!

What gift or gifts has Jesus given you that you can give back to Him?

PRAYER

Lord Jesus, show me how I can use the gifts You have given me for Your glory.

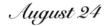

KEEP GROWING

Grace *to all who love our Lord
Jesus Christ with an undying love.*
Ephesians 6:24

What is your priority as a believer in Jesus Christ? There are many good answers, but I think this verse tells us that our priority must be to love Him more at the end of our life than we do now. To grow in our relationship with Him so we know Him better, trust Him more, and love Him more. To love Him when things are going well and when they are not. To love Him when we feel like it and when we don't. To love Him when He answers our prayers and when He doesn't. To love Him more with each passing year so when our lives are ending, we can say our love for Jesus is stronger than ever. Keep growing on your journey of faith until Jesus takes you Home.

Is your love for Jesus growing with each passing year? If not, what changes can you make?

PRAYER

Lord Jesus, I want my love for You to deepen each year. Help me draw closer to You so it will.

THE RIGHT ANSWER

Let your conversation always be
*full of **grace**, seasoned with salt, so that*
you may know how to answer everyone.
Colossians 4:6

There is nothing more confusing for an unbeliever than to hear a believer gossip about someone else, use God's name in vain, or use foul language. Rather than standing apart from the world, that kind of behavior is the world.

Paul uses salt as an example of how our conversations should be, because salt preserves and salt adds flavor. We are to preserve the integrity of our faith. Our words should be thoughtful, tasteful, and appropriate. They should enhance the conversation not diminish it, edify instead of criticize, support rather than undermine our identity as a Christian, draw people toward Christ not drive them away. When we speak with God's grace, He will always provide the right answer to the questions people have about Him.

How careful are you in your conversations not to confuse or hinder an unbeliever from coming to faith in Christ?

PRAYER

Lord Jesus, help my conversations be full of grace so I have the right answers for those who come to me.

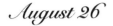

ONLY JESUS!

*Let us then approach the throne of **grace**
with confidence, so that we may receive mercy
and find **grace** to help us in our time of need.*
Hebrews 4:16

J esus lived on this earth as one of us, so He could identify with us and help us accordingly. There is nothing we will ever go through that He did not experience. He knew more hurt, pain, temptation, opposition, rejection, and betrayal than any of us will ever know. And today He sits in Heaven as our Great High Priest always interceding on our behalf.

No other gods could ever have such intimate involvement with us. No other gods left their thrones to be with us. No other gods are praying for us. Only Jesus! Therefore, we can approach Him with confidence because He knows us better than we know ourselves, and He alone has the mercy and grace to help us.

What do you need Jesus' help with today?

PRAYER

Lord Jesus, help me approach Your Throne with confidence. I need Your mercy and Your grace.

August 27

USE YOUR GIFT

*Each one should use whatever gift he has received to serve others, faithfully administering God's **grace** in its various forms.*
1 Peter 4:10

God's gifts to believers are different than the talents and abilities we are born with. They are also different than the fruit of His Spirit we are to cultivate. He gives believers certain gifts to strengthen His Church. It is up to us to determine our gift or gifts and use them for that purpose and His glory.

One of my youngest daughter's gifts is hospitality. She makes preparing dinner for her young adult Bible Study group every week look easy. She loves doing it, they love enjoying it, and God smiles because she is faithfully administering His grace to these young people on His behalf. Everyone benefits. Ask God to show you your gifts so you can do the same.

Have you asked God to show you His gifts so you can use them for Him?

PRAYER

Lord Jesus, help me know and use Your gifts for You.

GROW UP

---

*But grow in the **grace** and knowledge
of our Lord and Savior Jesus Christ.
2 Peter 3:18*

C hristians become ineffective for Jesus when we stall in our journey of faith; when we stagnate instead of move forward; when we remain in one place, so we go no place; when we are complacent, so we are spiritually impotent. Satan loves to keep us there, and he will do anything to hinder our desire or determination to read, study, pray, go to church, join a Bible study, or even meet other believers for fellowship. Suddenly vacuuming the house or cleaning the bathroom or checking our text messages seems more important.

But we must grow up in our faith. We must discipline ourselves so we will. We must go forward and grow in the grace and knowledge of our Lord and Savior Jesus Christ. He didn't save us for anything less.

What are you doing to grow up in your faith, so you don't stall or become complacent?

PRAYER

Lord Jesus, help me be diligent and disciplined in the study of Your Word, so I grow up in my faith.

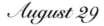

August 29

NO CHEAP GRACE

*They are godless men, who change the **grace**
of our God into a license for immorality and deny
Jesus Christ our only Sovereign and Lord.*
Jude 4

Have you ever handed the clerk at your grocery store a one-hundred-dollar bill and had her hold it up to see if it was real? Apparently certain markings reveal if it's fake.

The same is true in the Church. There are people who go through the motions and profess to believe in Jesus, but nothing changes in their life to prove it. In fact, their life reveals the opposite. They continue to do as they please. They hide behind the notion that God's grace will cover them, when in reality, God's grace saves us from sin, not so we can continue to sin. We know our salvation is genuine when we obey Jesus as our only Sovereign and Lord. There is no such thing as cheap grace.

Is there an area in your life where you are taking advantage of God's grace?

PRAYER

Lord Jesus, help me be genuine in my faith and never take Your grace for granted.

August 30

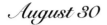

THE GREAT "I AM"

Grace *and peace to you from him who is,*
and who was, and who is to come.
Revelation 1:4

When God called Moses to lead the Israelites out of Egypt, He told Moses to tell them I AM had sent him (Exodus 3:14). It was a powerful moment. God was telling the world that He is not the I WAS God or the I WILL God but the I AM God. He is the God of the past because He controlled it, and He is the God of the future because He controls it, but if He isn't the God of the present, does it really matter?

We need to know God is with us now. We need to be able to trust Him now. We need His grace and peace now. His presence will always be with us, until we see Him face to face and can thank Him for being the great I AM.

How are you depending on God in your present circumstances?

PRAYER

Lord Jesus, You have helped me in the past, and You will help me in the future. Please help me now.

GOD'S AMAZING GRACE

*The **grace** of the Lord Jesus*
Christ be with God's people. Amen
Revelation 22:21

How fitting it is that these are the last words in the Bible. We need God's grace going forward, perhaps like never before, as our world is in chaos and seems to be spiraling out of control. But as God's people, we know it is not out of control because He is in control.

To quote the hymn "Amazing Grace" once again, we know, "His grace has led us safe thus far and His grace will lead us home." What a comfort it is to know that truth, trust that truth, live by that truth, and experience that truth on a daily basis for the rest of our lives. God's grace sent Jesus to save us from our sin so we could spend eternity with Him. Thank You, God, for Your amazing grace.

How will you thank God for His grace to you today?

PRAYER

Lord Jesus, help my life be an expression of gratitude for Your amazing grace.

September

MERCY

Look for God's **mercy**
on your journey of faith.

ASK FOR IT

---

*I will have **mercy** on whom I will have **mercy**, and I will have compassion on whom I will have compassion.*
Exodus 33:19

Mercy is a beautiful word. It means to refrain from harming or punishing offenders, enemies, or people in our power; a disposition to forgive, pity, be kind, compassionate, relieve suffering; clemency, blessing. A perfect description of our God.

We don't deserve God's forgiveness or kindness or compassion. We don't deserve His clemency or blessing. We deserve what He has the power to give us—eternal punishment for our sins. But in His mercy, He rescued us from such a fate. He holds our future in His hands. As we continue our journey of faith, ask Him for His mercy. He wants to know you want it, and He's ready and willing to give it to you. Ask for it.

Have you come to Christ with your sins and received God's mercy and forgiveness?

PRAYER

Lord Jesus, thank You for Your forgiveness and mercy through Jesus Christ.

September 2

BEG FOR IT

*Let us fall into the hands of the Lord,
for his **mercy** is great.*
2 Samuel 24:14

Sometimes all we can do is beg for God's mercy. When I was out of town and our oldest daughter was facing emergency surgery for a life-threatening illness, that's all I could do. I fell on my face before the Lord and begged.

We will never know this side of Heaven why God answers some of our prayers the way we want and why He doesn't, but that isn't for us to know. We are to ask and sometimes beg and then trust Him with the outcome. My daughter came through that emergency and we were greatly relieved. But there is always another one right around the corner. Let us remember to fall into the hands of the Lord and beg for His mercy.

What is your first response in times of crisis?

PRAYER

Lord Jesus, help my first response in a crisis be to fall into Your hands and beg for Your mercy.

DON'T TEST IT

---

*But in your great **mercy** you did not put
an end to them or abandon them, for you
are a great and **merciful** God.*
Nehemiah 9:31

G od had every right and justification to abandon the Israelites because of their continued defiance and disobedience. He had called them to be His people, but they consistently turned their backs on this privilege, even to the point of worshiping other gods. Why didn't He give up on them and choose another nation to be His, another people to worship Him? Because He had made a covenant promise with Abraham (Genesis 12:1-3).

God never breaks His promises. His mercy collided with the offense and the Israelites were spared. And we are forever grateful, because they gave us Jesus. We serve a great and merciful God. Let's don't test Him by being disobedient and expecting His mercy anyway.

Are you testing God's mercy today?

PRAYER

Lord Jesus, help me live in obedience to You so I am not testing Your mercy.

CALL HIM LORD

*Remember, O Lord, your great **mercy***
and love, for they are from old.
Psalm 25:6

We first see God's mercy in the Garden of Eden. Adam and Eve had disobeyed Him and deserved eternal punishment. Instead, God promised to send a Savior to take it for them (Genesis 3:15).

Where would we be without God's mercy? Without God's mercy, we would receive the punishment we deserve. There would be no escape, no alternative. Without God's mercy, we would live without hope in a world that is hopeless without Him. But because of His mercy, we are free to live the life He created us to live and our eternal future is secure. His love and mercy cancel the debt we owe for our sin. He earned the right to be our Lord.

Is Jesus the Lord of your life as well as the Savior of your life?

PRAYER

Thank You Jesus that because of Your mercy and love, I can call You Lord.

HE HEARS

Praise be to the Lord, for he
*as heard my cry for **mercy**.*
Psalm 28:6

As we listen to the news and watch what is going on in our world, we cry out to the Lord for mercy. It is heartbreaking to see our cities looted and vandalized, our monuments destroyed, our flag burned, and our Pledge of Allegiance mocked. I am participating in daily prayer for our country because I know God hears our prayers. He already has!

While evil will always be with us, it makes us grateful to see people cleaning up the messes, protecting the monuments, waving our flag, and saying the Pledge of Allegiance with their hand over their heart. And we can't help but say, "Thank You Lord." We praise Him because He heard our cry for mercy, and His mercy is more powerful than sin.

How are you praising God for the mercy He has shown you?

PRAYER

Lord Jesus, help me be just as quick to thank You for Your mercy as I am to ask for it.

September 6

TAKE REFUGE

---

*Have **mercy** on me, O God, have mercy on me,*
for in you my soul takes refuge.
Psalm 57:1

Where do we find refuge when our world is falling apart, when our kids rebel, our spouse leaves, we get a bad diagnosis, our parents need us? The old saying "It never rains but it pours" can be so accurate. If we don't have a plan in place for such times, we will be caught off guard and left defenseless. We will be overwhelmed by the stress of it all.

But God knew such times would come. And in His mercy, He has the plan to help us. He is our refuge. He is where our soul is quieted and strengthened and nourished and restored and equipped to handle what comes our way. He is our refuge, because He created us to need Him, and He is there when we do.

Where or what is your refuge when you are overwhelmed?

PRAYER

Lord Jesus, help me turn to You as the place of refuge I need when stress overwhelms me.

FIND MERCY

*He who conceals his sins does not prosper, but whoever confesses and renounces them finds **mercy**.*
Proverbs 28:13

David knew the truth of this verse firsthand. He had tried to hide his sin with Bathsheba, but he was miserable. His family was threatened, His country was threatened, and God's plan was threatened.

In His mercy, God doesn't let His people be comfortable in sin. He uses our conscience like a warning light in our car telling us to put our seat belt on. The light doesn't go off until we do. God nudges our conscience in the same way, because He doesn't like us to be miserable in our sin, and He can't use us when we are. So the warning light stays on until we confess our sin. Then, phew! We find mercy!

What sin is keeping you miserable and unusable to God?

PRAYER

Lord Jesus, help me confess my sin. I am ready to find Your mercy.

September 8

❧

BE CARRIED

---

*In all their distress he too was distressed. . . . In his love
and **mercy** he redeemed them; he lifted them up
and carried them all the days of old.*
Isaiah 63:9

G od did not create us to be distressed. We could say our distress distresses Him. It is contrary to His perfect design for us. Perhaps Isaiah is thinking of the time the Israelites were suffering in Egypt, and God sent Moses to lead them out.

But we can bring this verse closer to home and think of when we were suffering without God. In His love and mercy, He redeemed us or bought us back from the world of sin. He lifted us up and carried us—just like He did the Israelites— and He continues to carry us. How fortunate we are to have a God who loves us so tenderly, so intimately, and so compassionately. His love and His mercy are with us all the days of our lives. Let Him carry you.

What are you distressed about, and will you let Jesus carry you through it?

PRAYER

Lord Jesus, thank You that You are always with me and willing to carry me. Please carry me now.

September 9

ENJOY

*It is of the Lord's **mercies**
that we are not consumed. . . .
They are new every morning.*
Lamentations 3:22-23 (KJV)

We may not be aware of it, understand it or believe it, but we are completely dependent on God's mercy. We would be consumed without it. Good thing we get a fresh supply every day.

The Israelites spent forty years wandering in the wilderness because of their disobedience, but instead of having to hunt, kill, and cook their food, in His mercy, God sent a fresh batch of manna every morning. They didn't have to wonder where it was coming from, they didn't have to shop for it or go online and order it. They didn't have to do anything but wake up, enjoy it, and praise God for it. What a great way to start our day. Look for His mercies and enjoy.

Are you looking for God's mercies every morning? If not, will you start?

PRAYER

Lord Jesus, help me look for Your mercies each day and thank You for them.

September 10

MAKE YOUR REQUEST

We do not make requests of you because we are
righteous, but because of your great **mercy.**
Daniel 9:18

There is nothing in us that qualifies us to ask God for any-thing. Only through the righteousness of Jesus Christ do we dare come before a Holy and Perfect God and plead our cause and ask for His help. Only in Him are we qualified. Only in Him do we have the right credentials. The separation between God's holiness and our sinfulness creates a barrier we simply cannot cross.

Jesus crossed the barrier for us. Jesus made reconciliation with God possible. We can now stand before His Father clothed in His righteousness and make our requests known. This is God's great mercy to us and our rightful inheritance. Make your request with confidence. You are a child of God.

Are you covered with the righteousness of Jesus Christ, so you are qualified to stand before His Father and make your requests?

PRAYER

Lord Jesus, thank You for Your righteousness. Father, hear my prayer in Jesus' name.

SHOW MERCY

*For I desire **mercy**, not sacrifice,*
and acknowledgment of God
rather than burnt offerings.
Hosea 6:6

G od wants all of us—not just part of us. He doesn't want our token faith. He wants our faithfulness. He doesn't want our superficial religious behavior. He wants a genuine relationship. And He wants that relationship to bear out in our lives.

God cares more about how we live our faith than what we think we are sacrificing for our faith. He wants His mercy to us to multiply out to others. We will never impress God with our offerings or self-righteous sacrifices, but we can impress others by extending His mercy to them. This pleases God because it makes Him known and draws people to Him. Show mercy.

Whom can you show God's mercy to?

PRAYER

Lord Jesus, thank You for extending Your mercy to me. Help me extend it to someone else on Your behalf.

September 12

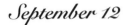

WALK HUMBLY

*And what does the Lord require of you? To act justly and to love **mercy** and to walk humbly with your God.*
Micah 6:8

As we watch the news unfold in our country, we see anything but justice, mercy, and humility. In fact, we see the total opposites. We see corruption in our federal and state governments that promote and protect injustice rather than justice. We see blatant lawlessness destroy the lives of innocent people. We see government leaders care more about their own political power than the needs of the people they are elected to serve.

God expects more from His people. He expects us to treat others the way He has treated us. He is our Supreme Leader, and we will only succeed as a people and as a nation when we do what He requires. Walk humbly before Him.

What are you doing to make sure you walk humbly before God?

PRAYER

Lord Jesus, help me stay close to You and obey Your Word so I do what You require and act justly, love mercy, and walk humbly before You.

September 13

NO OTHER GOD

*Who is a God like you? . . .
You do not stay angry forever
but delight to show **mercy**.*
Micah 7:18

My husband used to say that it took a lot to make his mother angry. But she had a slow smoldering type of anger that you didn't detect until it reached the boiling point and then, look out! As he would say, then she lowered the boom! And everything she had been mad about for months suddenly came pouring out.

Aren't we glad God doesn't do that with us? Yes, God is angry at our sin, but He never turns His anger on us. His ultimate act of love and mercy was sending Jesus to take our sins upon Himself. He took the wrath we deserve, and God could no longer stay angry. He delights in showing us His mercy. There is no other God like Him.

Do you have a slow, smoldering anger? A short fuse? How can you diffuse it and show mercy instead?

PRAYER

Lord Jesus, help me follow Your example and delight to show mercy instead of anger.

September 14

REMEMBER

*Lord, I have heard of your fame; I stand in awe of your
deeds, O Lord. Renew them in our day, in our time
make them known; in wrath remember **mercy**.*
Habakkuk 3:2

God gave the prophet Habakkuk the difficult assignment of warning Israel that they better turn back to
God or else! It seemed like an impossible task, so Habakkuk
did what we should do when we face a difficult situation—
remember who God is, remember what He has done, and
trust He will act on our behalf.

Reminding ourselves of God's power gives us confidence
He will display it again. Reminding ourselves of His mercy
gives us patience to keep asking until He does. And
acknowledging God's just anger reminds Him that we
know our place before Him. Remember!

The next time you face a difficult task, will you remember
who God is?

PRAYER

Lord Jesus, help me remember who You are and what You
have done in the past, so I trust You more in the present.

TRUE JUSTICE

*This is what the Lord Almighty says: "Administer true justice; show **mercy** and compassion to one another."*
Zechariah 7:9

D NA testing today is helping us achieve true justice. It has allowed us to re-open cases that are decades old and re-examine the evidence using the person's DNA to prove guilt or innocence.

A recent case told of a man who spent thirty-four years in prison for a crime his DNA test proved he did not commit. Instead of being bitter and in despair over such a fate, this man used his time to develop a singing talent he never knew he had. Upon his release, he shared his talent with the world and everyone who heard it was blessed. He received true justice and turned his injustice into a display of God's mercy and compassion. True justice always wins.

How have you been unjustly treated and what was your reaction?

PRAYER

Lord Jesus, help me be aware when people are mistreated and do what I can with compassion and mercy.

September 16

JESUS' WAY

*Blessed are the **merciful**,*
*for they shall be shown **mercy**.*
Matthew 5:7

Mercy is so important to God that Jesus included it in His famous Sermon on the Mount. It is one of eight declarations of blessings God bestows on His people when they obey His teaching.

The word *blessed* means to make happy or blissful; to be consecrated. And indeed, we are happy, blissful, and consecrated when we show God's mercy, because we are acting on His behalf. We are extending His work here on earth. We are showing Him off to a world that is harsh and cruel. We are showing the world there is another way, a better way—Jesus' way. And in return, we just receive more mercy because He never runs out.

Have you received the blessing of being merciful to someone?

PRAYER

Lord Jesus, show me in what situation and to whom I can show Your mercy today.

September 17

PRICELESS MERCY

Learn what this means:
*"I desire **mercy**, not sacrifice."*
Matthew 9:13

T he religious leaders of Jesus' day thought they were righteous because they strictly followed their own man-made laws. Jesus quotes the Old Testament prophet Hosea to set them straight (Hosea 6:6). Jesus calls this type of self-serving righteousness a worthless sacrifice, because it is superficial. It is fake worship, it is hypocritical, and God sees through both.

God desires mercy, because He is a God of mercy. Mercy defines Him, and it should define His people. We can't fake mercy, because mercy is His for us to give. Our self-centered sacrifices are worthless. His mercy is priceless.

What worthless sacrifice are you offering God instead of His mercy?

PRAYER

Lord Jesus, please reveal my worthless sacrifices and help me extend Your mercy instead.

September 18

❧

PROVE IT

*Shouldn't you have had **mercy** on
your fellow servant just as I had on you?*
Matthew 18:33

When we choose to follow Jesus Christ, all His attributes are at our disposal. We have access to them because we have access to Him. He loves us, therefore we can love Him. He is faithful to us, therefore we can be faithful to Him. He is holy, therefore we can be holy. He is merciful, therefore we can be merciful. We can pass His goodness on because His goodness resides in us. It is only our sinful nature that also resides in us that keeps us from being like Jesus. It's up to us whom we want to listen to and obey—His Holy Spirit who is always calling us to be like Him, or our sinful spirit that is always calling us not to be. Let your actions prove whom you listen to.

Whose voice do you listen to and obey, yours or the Holy Spirit's in you?

PRAYER

Lord Jesus, help me silence my own voice and listen to Yours, so I become more like You.

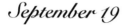

September 19

UNTIL HE RETURNS

---

*His **mercy** extends to those who fear him,*
from generation to generation.
Luke 1:50

The young virgin Mary sang these words of praise to God after she was told she would deliver His Son. We can hear her confidence and feel her joy. She was only a teenager from a poor family in an obscure village, but suddenly she could look beyond her own physical, educational, and geographical limitations to the impact the baby in her womb would have on humanity. Suddenly she could see what God saw. Everything in her life took on new meaning. Ours as well.

My second granddaughter just found out she is pregnant. Imagine her child being the recipient of God's mercy two thousand years later—from generation to generation until He returns.

How will you praise God for His mercy in your life today?

PRAYER

Lord Jesus, give me eyes to see Your mercy in my life. Help me to thank You for it each day.

September 20

ASK AND RECEIVE
---

*God, have **mercy** on me, a sinner.*
Luke 18:13

Some people don't think they need Jesus, because they don't think they sin. But even thinking they don't sin is sin, because God says we do (Romans 3:23). Until we see ourselves as He sees us, we are separated from Him with no chance for reconciliation. We are dead in our trespasses and sins (Ephesians 2:1).

The tax collector in this verse made no excuse for his sin, and he didn't offer a litany of good works in his defense. He came to Jesus with his sin and pleaded for His mercy. He instinctively knew he had wronged God, and he instinctively knew he was standing before Him now. So, he bowed before Him and asked for and received His mercy.

What is your attitude when you sin?

PRAYER

Lord Jesus, help me be honest before You when I sin, so I can receive Your mercy.

September 21

ONLY AT THE CROSS

*For God has bound all men over to disobedience
so that he may have **mercy** on them all.*
Romans 11:32

No matter our ethnic, racial, economic, political, educational, or religious background, we are all in bondage to our sin and headed in the wrong direction—until we come to Jesus. Sin is a universal problem, but salvation is an individual gift given to those who know their need, and meet Him at the cross for His mercy.

The cross stands in the middle of human history and beckons us to it. The Old Testament points forward to the cross, and the New Testament looks back to the cross, so that all people from every generation and every nation, nationality, language, and culture may be saved. God's mercy is available to all, but only at the cross.

With whom can you share this good news of God's mercy, so they can be saved?

PRAYER

Lord Jesus, thank You for Your mercy. Help me lead others to Your cross to find it.

September 22

LIVE FOR HIM

*Therefore, I urge you brothers, in view of God's **mercy**,
to offer your bodies as living sacrifices, holy and
pleasing to God—this is your spiritual act of worship.*
Romans 12:1

I f you were God, what would you think an appropriate response would be to all He has done for you? Paul must have thought about this question long and hard, because he came up with the most logical answer. We should give Him ourselves.

God is intimate, caring, and responsive. He wants us to be the same. The time for animal sacrifices is over. God is done with dead sacrifices. His Holy Spirit living in us allows us to offer Him ourselves as living sacrifices. He doesn't just want our external forms of worship. He wants our heart, mind, and will to want to live for Him. It's the best answer to our question, because it is our spiritual act of worship. Live for Him.

Have you given your heart, mind, and will to Jesus?

PRAYER

Lord Jesus, help me live for You as my spiritual act of worship.

GAIN HEART

---

*Therefore, since through God's **mercy***
we have this ministry, we do not lose heart.
2 Corinthians 4:1

My friend Margaret turned eighty this month. We always celebrate together, but of course this year everything is different because of the pandemic. She is a perfect example for this verse. She has taught women's Bible study groups, served as a deacon and an elder in her church, been a spiritual advisor to many, been a chaplain and volunteered her time in hospitals and nursing homes. And if that wasn't enough, she became an ordained minister. Retirement isn't in her vocabulary, so she continues on. She knows it is God's mercy working through her, so why would she lose heart?

Let's not lose heart either. Not everyone is called to be a Margaret, but all believers are called to do something for the Lord. Let's gain heart and continue on.

Where are you tempted to lose heart in your work for God?

PRAYER

Lord Jesus, please help me gain heart as I continue my journey of faith and work for You.

COME ALIVE IN JESUS

*God, who is rich in **mercy**,*
made us alive with Christ even when
we were dead in transgressions.
Ephesians 2:4-5

We are dead in our transgressions because sin kills us. Sin kills our bodies, our minds, our spirits, and our souls. Sin destroys our life on earth and destines us to eternity in Hell. But God loves to make dead things alive. Jesus' resurrection from the dead, after being in a guarded tomb for three days, proves it. He raised His own Son to demonstrate the power He has over sin, death, the devil, and Hell.

We don't have to stay dead in our transgressions. In His mercy, God makes us alive in Christ. He has a life for us to live, and we can't live it if we are walking around dead in our sins. Live the life He created you to live. Come alive in Jesus.

Are you still walking around dead in your transgressions?

PRAYER

Lord Jesus, thank You for taking my sins upon Yourself so I can have life in You.

September 25

GET SMART IN JESUS

*I was shown **mercy** because*
I acted in ignorance and unbelief.
1 Timothy 1:13

We are all ignorant until we come to saving faith in Jesus Christ. We are ignorant of God. We are ignorant of ourselves. We are ignorant of our desperate state without Him. We are ignorant of His Word, which teaches us how to know and live for Him, so we can spend eternity with Him.

It is one thing to be ignorant of the things of this world, because we are only here for a short while. But to be ignorant of the things of God has eternal consequences. Paul acted in ignorance and unbelief until he met Jesus. We all do. In His mercy, Jesus calls us all out of our ignorance and unbelief, because knowing Him makes us smart in His eyes. Get smart in Jesus.

What state of ignorance and unbelief has God called you out of?

PRAYER

Lord Jesus, thank You for calling me out of my ignorance and unbelief, so I can know You and be smart in You.

༼ঔ

TRUST HIS MERCY

*May the Lord show **mercy**
to the household of . . .*
2 Timothy 1:16

As the surviving matriarch of my family, I take my responsibility seriously. While I love to do things with and for my family, I know the most important thing I can do for them is pray. So each morning I name them one by one before God and ask Him to watch over them and draw them to Himself. I ask for His mercy, because at the end of the day, that is all we have to cling to.

We cannot control the myriad of events or circumstances that flood our families' lives, but we can depend on the One who does. We can pray this simple prayer like Paul did, "Lord, show mercy to my household," and then trust that He will, because He is the God of mercy. Trust His mercy.

Are you praying for your family and trusting God's mercy in their lives?

PRAYER

Lord Jesus, help me ask for and then trust Your mercy for my family.

September 27

GO TO THE THRONE

*Let us then approach the throne of grace with
confidence, so that we may receive **mercy** and
find grace to help us in our time of need.*
Hebrews 4:16

These are strange times. COVID-19 is isolating us and
as I write this, there is no end in sight. We can't be in
groups bigger than five, we have to keep six feet apart,
we have to wear face masks everywhere we go, and we
can't go to church.

But thank the Lord, because of Jesus, we don't need to be
together, or wear a face mask, or even be in church. We
have direct access to the Throne of God, because Jesus
broke down the barrier separating us. The moment Jesus
died on the cross, the massive curtain in the Temple was
torn from top to bottom telling the world the door is open
(Matthew 27:51). We can approach God with confidence.
Go to the Throne and receive His mercy and grace.

What do you need God's mercy and grace for today? Ask
Him for it.

PRAYER

Lord Jesus, thank You for breaking the barrier down so I can
approach God with confidence.

September 28

LET'S TAKE IT

*But the wisdom that comes from heaven is first of all pure; then peace-loving, considerate, submissive, full of **mercy** and good fruit, impartial and sincere.*
James 3:17

The world system apart from God lacks wisdom because God is wisdom. Apart from Him, we depend on our own limited resources which are always self-serving. The Bible says God's foolishness is wiser than our wisdom (1 Corinthians 1:25). So why would we ever depend on our own?

God's wisdom is pure, ours is impure; His is peace-loving, our is contentious; His is considerate, ours is selfish; His is submissive, ours is controlling; His is full of mercy, ours is 'show no mercy'; His bears good fruit, ours often bears rotten fruit; His is impartial, ours is biased; His is sincere, ours is pretentious. The God of Heaven wants to give us His wisdom. The choice is obvious! Let's take His wisdom over ours any day!

Whose wisdom are you depending on, yours or God's?

PRAYER

Lord Jesus, help me turn to You for Your wisdom because I have none without You.

September 29

BECAUSE HE LIVES . . .

---

*In his great **mercy** he has given us
new birth into a living hope through the
resurrection of Jesus Christ from the dead.*
1 Peter 1:3

The resurrection of Jesus Christ changed the world forever, and it changed us forever. It gave us a whole new perspective on life and death. This life is not all there is. We are not limited to our physical lifespan here on earth. In fact, this life is just a blip on the screen of eternity, and we will spend the rest of it either with God or separated from God.

In His mercy, God wants us to spend eternity with Him, and He sent Jesus so we could. Only Jesus gives us life in a dying world, and only Jesus gives us hope in a world without hope, because only Jesus is preparing a better life for us after this one is over. Because He lives, we live too, now and forever. That's the power of His resurrection. Even though it's September, we should celebrate Easter every day!

How does Jesus' resurrection change your perspective on life and death?

PRAYER

Lord Jesus, thank You for Your resurrection that guarantees mine when I believe in You.

RECEIVE HIS MERCY

Once you were not a people,
but now you are the people of God; once you
*had not received **mercy**, but now you have*
*received **mercy**.*
1 Peter 2:10

A ll believers have a before-and-after picture. A before-we-met-Jesus picture, and an after-we-met-Jesus picture. My 'before' picture was not pretty. I knew about Him, but I did not know Him. I was in a state of defiant disobedience until I got good and sick and ended up in the hospital. With my husband and four children under five at home, I needed God's mercy. I received it in that hospital room alone with Jesus, and my 'after' picture began.

Once I was not His, but now I am His. Once I did not want His mercy, now I depend on it. And not a day goes by I don't thank Him for it. It's the only way to live and the only way to die. Receive His mercy on your journey of faith.

What does your 'before' picture look like, and do you have an 'after' picture?

PRAYER

Lord Jesus, help me turn to You for Your mercy.

October

HOLINESS

Strive to be **holy** on your journey of faith.

BE HOLY

Although the whole earth is mine,
you will be for me a kingdom
*of priests and a **holy** nation.*
Exodus 19:5-6

We don't hear the word *holy* much today. It's counter to our twenty-first century thinking, because it means *belonging to or coming from God; consecrated, sacred, pure.* God called Israel to be a holy nation, separate from all other nations, as His vehicle through which He would send Jesus Christ into the world. Now God calls Christians to be separate from the world so we can minister to the world. He calls us to be holy because He is holy (1 Peter 1:16).

Holy also means *sound, whole, happy.* The world needs us to be holy. Our country needs us to be holy. Our families need us to be holy. As we continue our journey of faith, be holy and you will be happy in the process.

Have you given yourself to God, so He can make you holy?

PRAYER

Lord Jesus, I give myself to You so I can be holy in Your sight and useful in Your world.

✣

BE REFRESHED

*Remember the Sabbath
day by keeping it **holy**.*
Exodus 20:8

When God created the universe and the world we live in, He rested on the seventh day—not because He was tired or needed a break, but because He wanted to set an example for us. Part of the consequences of Adam and Eve's sin was that we would have to work for a living. God knew our bodies would get tired and our minds would get weary, so He tells us to take one day out of seven to rest, so we have time to catch up and be refreshed. Most of all, God wants us to take time to be refreshed in Him. This is not a suggestion; it's His fourth commandment. Sunday became our Sabbath after Jesus' resurrection. Keep it holy and be refreshed.

What do you do to keep Sunday, or another day in your week, set apart for God so He can refresh you?

PRAYER

Lord Jesus, help me honor Your command to set one day apart to be refreshed in You.

October 3

BE SEPARATE

*Consecrate yourselves and be **holy**, because I am the Lord your God. Keep my decrees and follow them. I am the Lord, who makes you **holy**.*
Leviticus 20:7-8

Bookstores are filled with self-help books because people basically want to improve themselves. We want to be better husbands, wives, parents, employers, workers, and students. We just want to be better! But "better" in God's eyes is holy, and only God can make us holy because we fall short. Only God can make us into the people He created us to be, and He gave us His Son, His written Word, and His Holy Spirit to help us.

The Bible is the bestselling book of all time, and the Ten Commandments are His decrees for us to follow. It is our job to know them, obey them, and teach them to our children. This separates us from the world around us and makes us holy before God. Be separate.

Do you turn to popular self-help books to be "better," or do you know and obey the Ten Commandments?

PRAYER

Lord Jesus, help me know and obey Your commandments. I want to be holy and separate for You.

October 4

PROTECT HIS NAME

*Do not profane my **holy** name.*
Leviticus 22:32

Do you ever wonder why people don't invoke the names of other gods when they swear instead of using God's name? Why don't we ever hear, "oh Buddha," or "oh Muhammad?" Could it be because those gods are worthless and have no power or control over anything, so what's the use?

That's exactly why God tells us emphatically not to profane His name, because He has all the power over everyone and everything. I grew up in a home where God's name was only used in vain. Even as a little girl, I knew it was wrong and always apologized to Him for it. God's name is holy. His third commandment tells us to keep it that way. Let's protect His name.

How careful are you never to profane God's name or Jesus' name?

PRAYER

Lord Jesus, You are holy. Help me never to profane Your name. I'm sorry for those who do, and I pray for their hearts to be changed.

THERE IS ONLY ONE

*He is a **holy** God; He is a jealous God.*
Joshua 24:19

God stands alone among all the ancient gods the Israelites were tempted to worship, and He stands alone among all the false gods we are tempted to worship. But no god, ancient or present, can compare to Him. Only God is holy and perfect in all His ways. Only God is the Almighty God, the Creator God, and the Sovereign God over all nations and all people.

No wonder He is also a jealous God. Why wouldn't He be? He demands our worship because He is the only God worth our worship. He is the only God who loves us and knows what is best for us. Let's give up the gods of our own making and worship the One who deserves it.

What gods of your own making are you tempted to worship over Almighty God?

PRAYER

Lord Jesus, help me hold You in the highest place in my life and worship You only.

October 6

REJOICE
---

*Glory in his **holy** name; let the hearts
of those who seek the Lord rejoice.*
1 Chronicles 16:10

S tress and anxiety are at an all-time high. We are threatened on all sides. Between the global pandemic, increased violence, and out of control lawlessness in our cities, the world is in chaos. People are desperate for relief.

One such city has been under siege for weeks and Christians have decided to take charge. Thousands gathered and started an old-fashioned revival in the midst of angry mobs attacking police and destroying property. The Christians won. Their hymns glorifying God silenced and dispersed the violent crowd. They were outnumbered and overpowered by the power of our holy God. Christians, let our voices be heard. Rejoice!

How are you standing with our holy God in the midst of the evil in our world?

PRAYER

Lord Jesus, help me stand with You, and show me how to stand against the evil in our world.

TRUST HIM

*Therefore my heart is glad and my tongue rejoices;
my body will also rest secure, because you
will not abandon me to the grave, nor will
you let your **Holy** One see decay.*
Psalm 16:9-10

David wrote these words when he was seeking refuge from his enemies. We all have enemies. Enemies of fear, insecurity, doubt, rejection, loneliness, despair. David turned away from his fears and turned to God for the security we all seek. He trusted God to take care of him in life and in death, and God gave him the vision of Jesus' resurrection from the dead to prove He would raise him too.

The antidote for fear is praise. We rejoice in God because He is bigger than all our fears. He makes our heart glad because we know we can trust Him to take care of us in this life and the next. Trust Him.

What is threatening your security today?

PRAYER

Lord Jesus, help me turn away from my fears and trust You for the security I seek.

October 8

♫

CLIMB HIGHER WITH JESUS

Who may ascend the hill of the Lord?
*Who may stand in his **holy** place?*
Psalm 24:3

Because God is holy, He requires us to be holy so we can be in His presence. But what does holy mean for us today? The same it has always meant. God's Word and God's standards do not change. David asked this question centuries before Christ and the next verse gives us the answer. It's the same today. Psalm 24:4 says personal holiness is having clean hands and a pure heart, having no idols, or swearing by what is false.

David couldn't make himself holy and neither can we. We can't stop sinning or want to stop sinning on our own. We can't give up the idols we worship over God on our own. We can't stop being deceitful or dishonest on our own. Only Jesus can make us holy. Let's climb higher with Jesus.

What sin do you need to give up so you can climb higher with Jesus?

_____

PRAYER

_____

Lord Jesus, help me turn from my sins so I can climb higher with You.

❦

CELEBATE GOD'S GREATNESS

*Your ways, O God, are **holy**.*
What god is so great as our God?
Psalm 77:13

Why doesn't God just let us be? Why doesn't He let us follow our own natural tendencies? Why does He expect so much of us when He knows we are only made of dust (Psalm 103:14)? This verse gives us the answer—because God is great.

God is not a little god who we can control to our own liking. He is not a god who lets us believe our own lies. His ways are holy, and His greatness calls us to be holy. He is a God who loves us too much to let us stay the way we are or follow our natural tendencies. He knows it would destroy us and keep us from being with Him for eternity. God's greatness saves us from ourselves. Celebrate God's greatness!

How has God shown His greatness to you?

PRAYER

Lord Jesus, Your ways are holy because You are a great God. Help me celebrate Your greatness in my life.

❦

PRAISE HIS NAME

The Lord reigns, let the nations tremble . . . let them
*praise your great and awesome name—he is **holy**.*
Psalm 99:1,3

In a world that is out of control, it's comforting to know that God is in control. He reigns over every nation and every ruler of every nation on earth. Nothing happens that He doesn't know about and control for His purpose and ultimate glory.

As the nations vie for power and supremacy, Jesus is in His holy Heaven moving history toward the time when He will return to rule this world as the King of kings and Lord of lords. The nations should tremble now because the day is coming when every knee will bow and every tongue confess Jesus is Lord (Philippians 2:10-11). Let's praise His holy name because He is coming soon!

In this world that seems so out of control, do you praise Him and rest in knowing He has it all under control?

PRAYER

Lord Jesus, I praise You for the comfort and security of knowing You are in control.

October 11

WORTH OUR WORSHIP

*Exalt the Lord our God and worship at his **holy** mountain, for the Lord our God is **holy**.*
Psalm 99:9

We worship what we think is worth our worship. Believers worship God because He has proven His worth. We worship Him because He makes Himself known. He made Himself known to Israel, and He makes Himself known to us in the Person of His Son Jesus Christ. We can know this God we worship. He is personally invested in our lives. We worship Him because He loves us, He forgives us, He saves us from our sins, He has a plan for our lives, He wants to spend eternity in His holy Heaven with us, and He is returning someday to take us there. We worship God because He is worth our worship.

How does your worship show God He is worth your worship?

PRAYER

Lord Jesus, help me worship You in a way that proves Your worth to me.

October 12

HOLY AND AWESOME

*He provided redemption for his people; he ordained his covenant forever—***holy*** and awesome is his name.*
Psalm 111:9

God is not a wishy-washy God. His actions toward us do not depend on our actions toward Him. They never have. He had chosen the Israelites to be His people even though He knew they would be rebellious, stiff-necked, stubborn, obstinate, and disobedient. But He had made a covenant with Abraham and that covenant would stand forever.

God's covenant with Abraham became His promise to us through Jesus Christ. In Him, God provided redemption from our sins. He redeemed us for Himself. God keeps His promises and we are forever the beneficiaries! Holy and awesome is His name.

How will you praise God for His holiness and thank Him for His awesomeness today?

PRAYER

Lord Jesus, You alone are holy and awesome. Help me praise and thank You for it every day!

SHOW HIM OFF

The Lord Almighty will be exalted
*by his justice, and the **holy** God will show*
*himself **holy** by his righteousness.*
Isaiah 5:16

We are seeing more injustice than justice today, more unholy than holy living, and more wrong behavior than right behavior. We live in a free-for-all society where everyone does what is right in their own eyes. Many consider God to be obsolete and irrelevant.

As a result, there is a great divide between the people who hold this worldview and Christians who hold to a biblical worldview. As long as God and His Word are denied, our culture will continue to self-destruct. Christians have to stand up for Jesus. He came to show us how to be just, how to be holy, and how to be righteous for our own good and survival. Let's exalt His name by showing Him off to the world.

How does your life reflect God's holiness, justice, and righteousness to a world that doesn't recognize Him?

PRAYER

Lord Jesus, help me show You off to a world that is desperate without You.

JOIN THE PRAISE

Holy, holy, holy *is the Lord Almighty;*
the whole earth is full of his glory.
Isaiah 6:3

Nothing is more reassuring than knowing with certainty who Jesus is, and that we can trust Him because of it. Seven centuries before He was born, Isaiah had this vision of Him sitting on His Throne in Heaven surrounded by angelic beings worshiping Him.

Isaiah recorded his experience so we can get a glimpse of what he saw. Otherwise we would never be able to imagine the majesty, the splendor, the power, the holiness, and the sheer glory that surrounds the Lord Jesus Christ. But He gave this vision to Isaiah to pass down to us to reassure us that all is well, because Jesus is on the Throne. Let's join this heavenly chorus and praise Him too.

How does knowing Jesus is on the Throne and in control reassure you today?

PRAYER

Lord Jesus, thank You for giving Isaiah this vision so I can join the heavenly voices and praise You too.

October 15

YOU DECIDE

"To whom will you compare me?
*Or who is my equal?" says the **Holy** One.*
Isaiah 40:25

The Israelites struggled in their relationship with God. Even though He had chosen them to be His people, they didn't always appreciate their calling. Even though He had proved Himself to be the One True God with His mighty power, they often worshiped the pagan gods of other nations rather than Him. They were fickle.

But people are fickle today too, and we can't be fickle with God. Either He is God and worthy of our total allegiance, or He is not. Either He is perfect and holy in all His ways, or He is not. Either He is completely trustworthy and worthy of our worship, or He is not. God poses the question to us, who is My equal? You decide.

How do you show God you are not fickle with Him because He is holy and perfect?

PRAYER

Lord Jesus, help me never be fickle in my relationship with You but give You my total allegiance.

October 16

QUESTIONS ANSWERED

For this is what the high and lofty
*One says—he who lives forever, whose name is **holy**:*
*"I live in a high and **holy** place."*
Isaiah 57:15

Do you look forward to going to Heaven? Do you wonder what it looks like? Do you wonder what we will do there? Most of all, do you wonder what it will be like to be with God and see Jesus face to face?

God only gives us glimpses of Heaven in His Word because He knows we can't possibly comprehend the magnificence, splendor, beauty, and perfection of it all. We can only take His Word for it. He lives in a high and lofty place, He is the high and lofty One, whose name is holy, and He invites us to live with Him. We don't have to wonder what Heaven will be like. If we know Jesus, we will spend eternity there, and all our questions will be answered.

What do you look forward to most about going to Heaven?

PRAYER

Lord Jesus, thank You for preparing this awesome place for us so we can be with You forever.

October 17

GATHERED WITH JESUS

*This is what the Sovereign Lord says: When I gather the people of Israel from the nations from where they have been scattered, I will show myself **holy** among them in the sight of the nations.*
Ezekiel 28:25

I srael is the only nation ever to be scattered from their homeland and brought together again. God saw to it, because He planned it that way. Israel will always be His chosen nation, and He will protect her until Jesus returns.

Like Israel, we are scattered until Jesus brings us together in Him. We are scattered in our thinking, our beliefs, and our values. We are at the mercy of the world's system and philosophy. We are in Satan's kingdom instead of God's kingdom. We are lost in sin with no way out. But the Lord says the same to us: I will gather you from where you have been scattered and show Myself holy. And when He does, we want to be holy too.

Are you scattered in your relationship with God? Let Him bring you together in Jesus.

PRAYER

Lord Jesus, please gather me to Yourself and show me Your holiness so I can be holy too.

❧

GIVE UP THE FALSE GODS

*But the Lord is in his **holy** temple;*
let all the earth be silent before him.
Habakkuk 2:20

What false gods are you tempted to worship? There are many to choose from. The gods of materialism, consumerism, success, status, prestige, selfish ambition, self-esteem. We worship them because we can fashion them to our own liking.

Israel was tempted to worship the false gods of other nations for the same reason—man-made gods of wood and stone that could neither hear nor speak. Habakkuk sounded the warning to them, and he sounds the warning to us. What good is a god that is impotent before you? Worship the Lord whose power and presence makes you stand in silence before Him. His holiness commands it. Give up the false gods.

What false gods are you tempted to worship? Are you willing to give them up?

PRAYER

Lord Jesus, help me give up the gods of my own making and worship You.

A STEP CLOSER

*Offer [your bodies] in slavery to
righteousness leading to **holiness**.*
Romans 6:19

We wake up every day with a clean slate before us. We can't always choose what the day will bring, but we can choose how we will respond. We can choose our attitude in response to our circumstances.

Starting our day with God gives His Holy Spirit permission to take the lead and show us the way. When we are tempted to react in frustration, He gives us patience. When we might react in anger, we have His calmness. When we are disappointed, He gives us hope. The Holy Spirit's job is to make believers more like Jesus. Our job is to let Him. Give your day to Jesus and watch how He leads you a step closer to holiness.

Do you start your day with Jesus? If not, will you?

PRAYER

Lord Jesus, help me start my days with You so I can watch You make me more like You.

October 20

❦

KNOW IT AND OBEY IT

*So then, the law is **holy**,*
*and the commandment is **holy**,*
righteous and good.
Romans 7:12

We live in a frightening time. Not just because of the COVID-19 pandemic, natural disasters, and violence in our cities. Those dangers are frightening enough, but our greatest fear should be turning away from God.

Public schools can no longer mention God's name and His Ten Commandments can no longer be posted. It's as if we are trying to eliminate Him by simply removing Him. But God will never be removed. Instead He will let us have our way. He will let us think we have removed Him and see how far we get. So far, not very far. Without God's law, we can't be holy. We can't be righteous. We can't even be good. God's law is for our good. It's in our interest to know it and obey it.

What is most frightening to you in today's world?

PRAYER

Lord Jesus, there's a lot to be afraid of today but my greatest fear is turning from You. Help me know and obey Your commandments so I don't.

❧

DON'T BE AFRAID
TO BE HOLY

Therefore, I urge you, brothers, in view of God's mercy,
*to offer your bodies as living sacrifices, **holy** and*
pleasing to God—this is your spiritual act of worship.
Romans 12:1

What comes to your mind when someone describes a person as holy? Religious? Rigid? Reclusive? Too good to be any fun? Unfortunately, being holy can have negative connotations to people.

But God means holy in the most positive sense. He wants us to live for Him. He wants our faith in Him to be a beacon of light and hope in a dark and hopeless world. He wants the world to want what we have. How can people want what we have when our behavior is no different than theirs? God wants us to be genuine, authentic, real, alive, and passionate in our relationship with Him. This pleases Him. It tells the world we worship Him. Don't be afraid to be holy.

How is your life holy and pleasing to God? How is it not?

PRAYER

Lord Jesus, I want my life to be holy and pleasing to You. Help me give myself to You so You can make it so.

❦

CLEAN IN AND OUT

*Let us purify ourselves from everything that contaminates body and spirit, perfecting **holiness** out of reverence for God.*
2 Corinthians 7:1

Being in the middle of a global pandemic has made us clean freaks! We don't go anywhere without our masks, our hand sanitizer, and our surgical gloves. It makes us wonder if we were this careful with the ordinary flu, could we lessen its effects and save lives?

The same is true for sin. If we took sin seriously and purified ourselves from its deadly contamination, could we lessen its effects and save lives for all eternity? Sin is in our DNA, so we will never eradicate it, and thank God, Jesus saves us from it. But we can eliminate the contaminants sin produces. We can purify ourselves. We can aspire to holy living and be clean in and out.

What sinful contaminant do you need to get rid of so you can be clean inside and outside?

PRAYER

Lord Jesus, help me purify myself from the contaminants that dirty my life. Help me be clean for You.

October 23

❧

RUN FROM TEMPTATION

*But among you there must not be even
a hint of sexual immorality, or of any kind of impurity,
or of greed, because these are improper
for God's **holy** people.*
Ephesians 5:3

The world bombards us with temptations, but sexual temptation probably tops the list. Satan is behind it and our screens make sure of it, because nothing destroys individuals, families, cities, and nations faster than sexual immorality. Impurity of any kind is the antithesis of holiness, and holiness should be the hallmark of every believer in Jesus Christ.

Holiness distinguishes believers from unbelievers in a world that wants a blended society. God does not call us to blend in but to stand out. Holiness sets us apart and tells the world we live for Him and not our own pleasures. Holiness proves our faith more than any other Christian trait. Run from the temptation. Be holy.

How quick are you to run from the temptations we all face?

PRAYER

Lord Jesus, help me run from temptation. I want to be holy before You.

MARVEL AT THE LORD

*On the day he comes to be glorified
in his **holy** people and to be marveled at
among all those who have believed.*
2 Thessalonians 1:10

The greatest day in our life is the day we receive Jesus Christ as our Lord and Savior. It separates every day after it from every day before it, because it changes us forever. Jesus becomes real to us and is glorified through us. Our new faith grows. We mature. We trust God with our lives and our circumstances. Other believers encourage us along the way, and we do the same. We are family and we take care of each other. We rejoice together and we mourn together. Most of all we marvel at the One who called us to Himself. And we never forget the day He did. Someday, we will all stand before Him and marvel at Him together!

How are you encouraging fellow believers in their faith the way you have been encouraged in yours?

PRAYER

Lord Jesus, thank You for those who have encouraged me along the way. Help me encourage others in their faith.

✍

PROUD TO BE A CHRISTIAN

Do not be ashamed to testify about our Lord . . .
*who has saved us and called us to a **holy** life—not*
because of anything we have done but because of
his own purpose and grace.
2 Timothy 1:8-9

It's our nature to want to be liked, popular, and respected. We are social creatures and we want and need friends. That makes it easy to go along with them, so we get along with them.

But when it comes to our faith, Jesus want us to stand up and stand out, so we make Him known. He includes us in His purpose of bringing others to Him. That means we have to be willing to be rejected like He was, not always popular with our friends like He was, and not respected but ridiculed for our beliefs like He was. We have to be proud to be a Christian and ready to tell people what He has done for us, so they can have Him too.

How prepared and bold are you in telling people about your faith in Christ?

PRAYER

Lord Jesus, thank You that someone was prepared to tell me about You. Help me do the same for someone else.

❧

READ THE DIRECTIONS

*You have known the **holy** Scriptures,*
which are able to make you wise for
salvation through faith in Christ Jesus.
2 Timothy 3:15

How many times have you tried to put something together or fix something and ended up frustrated in the process, because you didn't read the directions first? We've probably all heard the expression, "when all else fails, read the manual." That is never more true than when it comes to faith.

It is impossible to put ourselves together or fix the messes in our lives without following God's directions for us in the Bible. The Bible is God's Word to us. It is unique from every other book ever written, because it is His living Word, sacred, holy, without error, and applicable to every generation. It leads us to salvation and gives us wisdom going forward. To continue your journey of faith, read it first, not last.

How often do you read the Bible and what prompts you to read it?

PRAYER

Lord Jesus, help me read Your Word every day for the wisdom I need to live for You.

HIS PERSPECTIVE

God disciplines us for our own good,
that we may share in his **holiness.**
Hebrews 12:10

Do you ever wonder why some people have more problems than others? Do you ever wonder if God is favoring one over the other? The problem is not with God but with us.

Our idea of problems and suffering is different than God's. We associate it with His lack of favor when often, the opposite is true. God allows problems and suffering in our lives to draw us to Himself—to show us our weakness and His strength. No one will go through life trouble-free, because we live in a sin-filled world. We can accept the troubles that come our way, because God uses them to make us more like Him. We just need to see them from His perspective, not ours.

Do you see problems as interruptions or opportunities to be more like Jesus?

PRAYER

Lord Jesus, help me view problems from Your perspective instead of mine. Use them to make me more like You.

❧

BE A PEACEMAKER

*Make every effort to live in peace with all men and to be **holy**; without **holiness** no one will see the Lord.*
Hebrews 12:14

Our world is anything but peaceful. There is tension between nations, governments, cities, and people that has produced chaos, confusion, disruption, and lawlessness. We should be more sophisticated and more advanced in the twenty-first century, but it seems we have gone backward instead of forward. What is the answer? There is only one. His name is Jesus, and He is our only source of peace.

Jesus came to show us how to live peaceably in an unpeaceful world. His teaching, preaching, and example of holiness changed the world forever. The only way to have peace is for more of us to be more like Him. Be a peacemaker.

Is there chaos in your family? How can you be a peacemaker in the situation?

PRAYER

Lord Jesus, help me be like You and be a peacemaker in my world and in my family.

❦

ONLY HOLY IN JESUS

*But just as he who called you is **holy**, so be holy in all you do; for it is written: "Be **holy**, because I am **holy**."*
1 Peter 1:15-16

The Apostle Peter was anything but holy when he first met Jesus. Jesus called him anyway. He called Peter to leave his old life behind and follow Him to new heights, and Peter obeyed. He was mesmerized by Jesus' teaching and captivated by His love. Being with Jesus enabled Peter to go from being a crass and hot-tempered fisherman to a passionate preacher of the gospel and leader of the early Church.

Peter is proof that when Jesus calls us to follow Him, He changes us from the inside out. He calls us to shed the bad behaviors of our past and take on His. He calls us to be holy, and He's the only One who can make us so. Be holy in Jesus.

Do you consider yourself holy? Why or why not?

PRAYER

Lord Jesus, I want to be holy because You are holy. Change me so I am more like You.

SPEED HIS COMING

*You ought to live **holy** and godly lives as you look forward to the day of God and speed its coming.*
2 Peter 3:11-12

Every day we are closer to the day when Jesus Christ is coming back. How do we want Him to find us when He does? Do we want Him to find us living for ourselves and our own desires? Do we want Him to find us blending in with the world that opposes Him rather than living for Him? Do we want Him to be pleased with us when He returns instead of disappointed?

There is only one way to guarantee God's pleasure, and that's holiness. Holiness is choosing His way over our way. Holiness is looking forward to His coming more than seeking the temporary pleasures of this world. Holiness hastens His coming, because we can't wait. Speed His coming!

How do you want Jesus to find you when He returns?

PRAYER

Lord Jesus, help me choose to live a holy and godly life so I look forward to Your return.

GRATEFUL TO BE HOLY

Day and night they never stop saying:
*"**Holy, holy, holy** is the Lord God Almighty,*
who was, and is, and is to come."
Revelation 4:8

J ohn was exiled to the Island of Patmos for his faith. He was sent there to waste away and die. But God had other ideas. He told John to write the last book of our Bible which John called Revelation, because it reveals Jesus and God's plan for the world.

We can know the end of the story. We can know the God who was in the beginning creating the universe and every-thing in it. We can know the God who is with us in the present in the Person of His Son. And we can know the God of the future when Jesus returns to take us Home. We will gratefully join the heavenly chorus saying, "Holy, holy, holy is the Lord God Almighty!" because He made us holy too.

How do you show God your gratitude for calling you to be holy on your journey of faith?

PRAYER

Lord Jesus, thank You for Your holiness that makes me want to be holy too.

November

PRAYER

❧

Prayer is a privilege
on our journey of faith.

❧

GOD HEARS

*God heard them, for their **prayer***
reached heaven, his holy dwelling place.
2 Chronicles 30:27

N ot since the days of Solomon had the Israelites come together to celebrate Passover—when God freed them from Egyptian bondage. King Hezekiah changed that. He sent word for the people to meet in Jerusalem. There was much prayer and great rejoicing as they celebrated their past with Him and looked forward to their future. God was pleased and heard their prayer.

Prayer is our lifeline to God. Prayer tells Him we need Him, want Him, and depend on Him. Prayer has many forms—worship, thanksgiving, confession, petition. Whether we pray individually or with other believers, God hears it all. It's the perfect way to start November. Prayer is a priority on our journey of faith.

What place does prayer have in your life?

PRAYER

Lord Jesus, help me make prayer a priority because I need You and You hear me when I pray.

❧

GOD ANSWERS

*So we fasted and petitioned our God about this,
and he answered our **prayer**.*
Ezra 8:23

E zra teaches us about serious prayer, prayer that gets God's attention. Jews were returning from years of exile to their beloved Jerusalem. It was a dangerous journey. So they fasted and prayed. God answered their prayer and kept them safe.

God does the same for us when we give Him our undivided attention, when we take time away from something else to talk to Him, when we pray with sincerity and heart, when we pray without distraction and superficiality. Serious prayer requires fasting from something—time on social media, a program on TV, a phone call with a friend. God wants to know we are coming to Him because we know He loves us, is there for us, and has the power to help us. These are the prayers God answers.

What do you need to fast from so God knows you are serious in your prayers?

PRAYER

Lord Jesus, help me take prayer seriously.

IN JESUS' NAME

*O Lord, let your ear be attentive
to the **prayer** of this your servant and
to the prayer of your servants who
delight in revering your name.*
Nehemiah 1:11

A remnant of Jews had returned from exile, and Jerusalem was in ruins. Nehemiah heard the news and was distraught. But unlike people who hear bad news and feel bad for a moment or two, Nehemiah mourned, wept, fasted, and prayed. Then he took action. In record time, even by today's standard, the walls around Jerusalem were rebuilt and restoration of the city began.

Many of our cities are in ruins today. But God always has a 'Nehemiah' and people who revere His name ready to pray. Let's be those people now and pray for our nation and our cities in Jesus' name.

Are you praying for our nation and our cities? If we don't, who will?

PRAYER

Lord Jesus, help me take my responsibility seriously to pray for our nation and our cities.

❧

GOD IS BIG ENOUGH

Answer me when I call to you,
O my righteous God. Give me
release from my distress; be merciful
*to me and hear my **prayer**.*
Psalm 4:1

Let's face it, stress is the new normal in the twenty-first century. We search for relief in projects, busyness, exercise, vacations, food, shopping—the list continues, but so does our stress.

God didn't create us to live in stress because of its negative results. Stress keeps us anxious, worried, unsettled, and fearful. Stress can make us feel hopeless and depressed. Stress affects us physically, mentally, emotionally, and spiritually. Most of all, stress distracts us from God and His availability and desire to relieve it. Only God is big enough to carry all the stress of every single person on earth. Why not let Him carry ours?

Are you allowing God to carry your stress?

PRAYER

Lord Jesus, help me remember You are there to carry my stress so I don't have to.

IT'S OKAY TO BEG

The Lord has heard my cry for mercy;
*the Lord accepts my **prayer**.*
Psalm 6:9

Have you ever been on total overload and just called out to God for His mercy? We can all feel like we're in over our head at times, just like David when he wrote these words. He was in agony with a life-threatening illness and convinced he was going to die. His enemies were taking advantage of his weakness and all he could do was cling to God and beg for his mercy.

David's response is a great example for us when we are backed into a corner and overwhelmed by our circumstances. There are different responses for sure, but the best thing to do is find a quiet spot and just cry out to God. He knows what we are going through. He hears our desperateness. He is ready to help. It's okay to beg.

What situation are you in that you need God's mercy? Will you ask Him—no, beg Him—for it?

PRAYER

Lord Jesus, I am in over my head. I beg You for Your mercy today.

November 6

❧

BE HONEST—GOD KNOWS ANYWAY

*Hear, O Lord . . . give ear to my **prayer**—*
it does not come from deceitful lips.
Psalm 17:1

We cannot manipulate God. He is omniscient. He knows everything, so there is no use trying to keep anything from Him. He knows our ambitions, our attitudes, and our motives. He knows when they are honest and genuine and when they are not. He knows us as we really are, not how we pretend to be. So our prayers have to be sincere before Him.

We can't come to God with any other motive than humility and gratitude for His Supremacy. When we do, we can be confident like David was and say, "Give me Your ear Lord. Deceit hurts any relationship, and I don't want it to hurt ours." Be honest with God and He will hear your prayer.

How are you trying to manipulate God instead of surrendering to Him?

PRAYER

Lord Jesus, help me always be honest before You because You know when I am not.

SOAK IN HIS LOVE

By day the Lord directs his love,
*at night his song is with me—a **prayer***
to the God of my life.
Psalm 42:8

Our world has never felt more uncertain and insecure. Between the pandemic, threats from foreign enemies, and lawlessness in our cities, we need God, and we need to know we need Him. Only His love is powerful enough to overcome our fears and insecurities. Only His love can comfort us in a scary world. And it does.

God's love covers us like a warm blanket. We can snuggle into it and be reassured that everything will be all right. His love covers us during the day and follows us into the night. He is with us when we go to sleep and when we can't sleep. Those sleepless hours are a great time to pray and soak in His love. He is the God of our life and no one loves us like He does. Soak in His love.

How is God's love reassuring you in the scary world we live in?

PRAYER

Lord Jesus, thank You for being the God of my life and loving me like no one else can.

PRAISE FIRST

*May the peoples **praise** you, O God;*
*may all the peoples **praise** you.*
Psalm 67:3

P raise is the highest form of prayer. But all too often we go to God with what we need before telling Him why we need Him. Praise gets our priorities right. Praise establishes His rightful place and gives us the confidence to come to Him with our needs. Who doesn't like to be praised for who we are before being asked to do something? It tells us we are noticed and appreciated for what we have done in the past and can be trusted now.

God doesn't need our praise, but He wants our praise. He wants us to remember Who He is, because it helps us view our needs through His lens instead of ours. God is worthy of our highest praise. What a different world this would be if all the people praised Him—first!

Do you praise God as much as you pray to Him?

PRAYER

Lord Jesus, help me precede every prayer to You with praise for You and what You have done and are doing in my life.

IN THE WOMB

*From birth I have relied on you; you brought me forth
from my mother's womb. I will ever **praise** you.*
Psalm 71:6

My second granddaughter is pregnant with her first child. The first ultrasound at only 11 weeks shows the tiny fetus with legs kicking, arms outstretched, and a perfect profile. This baby cannot pray for itself right now, but it is surrounded by people who are. What a privilege to see this unborn child and pray he or she will receive the legacy of faith being passed on.

Science and medicine have proven that life begins at conception. It's our responsibility to praise God for this new life, so when that child is born, they will be used to hearing God praised and want to praise Him too—for the rest of their life. And we can spend the rest of our life praising Him for ours.

Do you see life in the womb as a life worth praying for? How will you praise Him for your life today?

PRAYER

Lord Jesus, help me praise You all the days of my life for giving me life.

November 10

❧

LOOK UP TO THE HEAVENS

*The heavens **praise** your wonders,*
O Lord . . . For who in the skies above
can compare with the Lord?
Psalm 89:5-6

When you don't know how to pray or what to say when you do, just go outside and look up! The psalmist said it well, "the heavens declare the glory of God" (Psalm 19:1). The sky is an ever-changing panorama displaying God's creative beauty and majesty. In our always-changing world, it represents His unchanging power and glory.

When we have no words, God gives us the words when we think about who He is and the power He has to keep everything in His universe in perfect harmony and balance, including us. So why not step outside and let Him speak to you, so you can speak back to Him. If nothing else, you can just stare in wonder because no one and nothing else can ever compare to Him. Look up!

How often do you go outside and look up and just praise God for His creation?

PRAYER

Lord Jesus, help me take time every day to look up to the heavens and praise You for Your creation.

BOOKENDS

*It is good to **praise** the Lord and make music to your name, O Most High, to proclaim your love in the morning and your faithfulness at night.*
Psalm 92:1-2

What better way to start our day than praising God for loving us and telling Him we love Him in return? Putting Him first sets the tone for our attitudes and controls our response to whatever the day brings. It reminds us we are in it together. Even when our day brings headaches and heartaches, God puts a song in our heart. He helps us stay centered and focused. When our work is done and it's time to tuck in for the night, we can look back and praise Him again, because no matter what came our way, He was there, and we can thank Him for His faithfulness. We can go to sleep thanking Him for His love that began our day and His faithfulness that ended it. We can thank Him for being the bookends on our day.

Will you make God the bookends to your day by praising Him for His love in the morning and His faithfulness before you go to sleep?

PRAYER

Lord Jesus, help me make prayer the bookends to my day.

BE RICH

*He will respond to the **prayer** of the destitute;*
he will not despise their plea.
Psalm 102:17

To be destitute is to be without the basic necessities of life. We are all destitute without Christ. He is the most basic need of our heart, mind, and soul. Augustine described it well when he said "our souls are restless until we find our rest in Thee." Without Christ, we are wandering through life trying to find our way. But He knows the way. We are fending for ourselves in a cruel and competitive world when He is there for us. He wants us to be rich, not destitute.

We can call out to Jesus and know that He hears our prayers and will help us. We can trust Him to heal our heart, feed our mind, and restore our soul. No problem will be too small or insignificant. No prayer will be unworthy of His attention. He does not want us to be destitute. He wants us to be rich!

How is Jesus filling the most basic needs of your heart, mind, and soul?

PRAYER

Lord Jesus, thank You for making me rich in You.

꙳

BE RIGHTEOUS

*The Lord is far from the wicked but
he hears the **prayer** of the righteous.*
Proverbs 15:29

God is a Gentleman. When we choose to separate our-selves from Him, He lets us be. But we do so at our own risk. He considers us wicked because we have rejected His Son's sacrifice on our behalf. We are evil and immoral in God's sight. There is no covering for our sin, and He is far from us.

But when we accept Jesus' sacrifice, we become recon-ciled to God, and He considers us righteous. We are heirs with Christ to all God's resources and blessings—our sins are forgiven, we are saved for all eternity, His Holy Spirit lives in us, and we have direct access to Him in prayer. We can be wicked or righteous. He gives us the freedom to choose. Choose to be righteous!

Does God consider you righteous in His sight because you made the right choice?

PRAYER

Lord Jesus, please hear my prayers because You make me righteous in Your sight.

MAKE IT A HABIT

[Daniel] prayed . . .
just as he had done before.
Daniel 6:10

I have heard it said that it takes thirty days to form a habit. If we want to stop a bad behavior or begin a good one, plan on doing it for a month so it becomes your new routine. It was Daniel's habit to pray. It was central to his life, so he prayed his way through. From being taken captive in Babylon as a teenager, to interpreting the king's dreams, to being delivered from the lion's den, to being given visions as an old man, Daniel prayed. And we have been blessed by his prayers.

Daniel's prayer life is a powerful example for us to pray our way through our own journey of faith. Daniel developed the habit of prayer and it sustained him and directed his life. It will do the same for us. Make prayer a habit.

Is it your habit to pray or is prayer your last resort?

PRAYER

Lord Jesus, help me make prayer a daily habit so I am blessed and so are those around me.

IT DOESN'T PAY TO DISOBEY

From inside the fish Jonah
prayed *to the Lord his God.*
Jonah 2:1

G od told Jonah to go to Nineveh and preach against the evil that had overtaken that great city. Jonah ran away. In fact, he went in the opposite direction, assuming God didn't notice and would find someone else. But God noticed, and Jonah paid a big price for his disobedience. He landed in the belly of a whale.

Some people believe the story of Jonah is just a fairytale, but there is no fiction in God's Word. Jonah describes his experience in detail—plunging to the depths of the ocean, seaweed wrapping around his neck, drowning, his life ebbing away. We can run away from God, but He never runs away from us. Jonah prayed, God heard, and the great fish threw him up on the beach. It doesn't pay to disobey!

Where or how are you running away from God right now? Think about Jonah.

PRAYER

Lord Jesus, I know I can't run away from You. Help me remember Jonah and obey You instead.

❧

MAKE IT HAPPEN

*When you **pray**, go into your room,*
*close the door and **pray** to your Father.*
Matthew 6:6

We know we can pray anytime, anywhere, but there is something extra special about going into our room, closing the door, and getting down on our knees to pray. We can only imagine the reaction of the huge crowd following Jesus when He told them to do this. They were used to seeing the Jewish religious leaders make a big scene when they prayed. They wanted to make sure everyone saw them and heard them. But Jesus called them hypocrites.

So Jesus says, let your prayer time be a special time just between you and God, and He will reward you because you are His child and He loves to spend that time with you. It's up to us to make it happen.

How often do you go in your room or some quiet place so you can be alone with God to pray?

PRAYER

Lord Jesus, help me look forward to spending time alone with You in prayer.

November 17

THE LORD'S PRAYER—PASS IT ON

*This, then, is how you should **pray**: "Our Father in heaven, hallowed be your name, your kingdom come, your will be done on earth as it is in heaven. Give us today our daily bread. Forgive us our debts, as we also have forgiven our debtors. And lead us not into temptation, but deliver us from the evil one."*
Matthew 6:9-13

After seeing Jesus pray, the disciples asked Jesus to teach them how to pray. He did, and believers have been praying this prayer ever since. Known as the Lord's Prayer, it covers all the bases. It tells us God is our Father, that He lives in Heaven, that He is sovereign over Heaven and earth, that He provides for us, that He forgives our sins and expects us to forgive others, and that He has ultimate power over Satan.

If we know and understand the Lord's Prayer, we are acknowledging Who God is and His sovereign power over His creation. We are putting ourselves in good hands. Let's be sure to pass this timelessly effective prayer on to our children and grandchildren, because it says it all. Pass it on.

Do you know and pray the Lord's Prayer yourself? Whom can you pray it with?

PRAYER

Lord Jesus, help me know and pray this prayer and pray it with others, especially my family.

❧

DON'T ROB GOD

*"My house will be called
a house of **prayer**," but you are
making it "a den of robbers."*
Matthew 21:13

C hurches are shut down because of COVID-19, but it hasn't stopped the Church from praying. God's people have always been resourceful. We find a way. Thanks to modern technology, we can livestream churches all over the country and join their worship, hear their sermons, and pray. In fact, I have been "attending" three different services each week and blessed by all three, because God's people come together and pray.

Prayer is essential in God's house. He wants us to pray together. He loves us to pray together. Prayer proves our worship of Him and our reliance on Him. We rob Him of that when we don't pray. We can always find a way to come together and pray. Let's don't rob God.

Would God call your church a house of prayer?

PRAYER

Lord Jesus, help me do my part to make sure my church is always a house of prayer.

∂⁄◯

PRAY AND BELIEVE

If you believe, you will receive
*whatever you ask for in **prayer**.*
Matthew 21:22

What does this verse mean exactly? Does it mean God won't answer my prayer if I don't believe He will? Does it mean I am not praying right or praying long enough? Jesus spoke these words to the disciples when He cursed a fig tree for not bearing fruit. Immediately the fig tree withered and died. The disciples were stunned and wondered how this could happen. Jesus said, "If you believe, you can do it too." But who wants to curse a fig tree?

Jesus is using this extreme comparison to teach the disciples, and us, that we will receive what we ask for when our prayers align with Him. His answer may come quickly, or it may take years, maybe even beyond our lifetime. But it will happen, because God wants it too. Pray and believe!

What are you praying for that you have not yet received? Make sure it aligns with God and His Word, and then believe.

PRAYER

Lord Jesus, help me trust You for what I am praying for because I know You want it too.

MAKE TIME FOR GOD

*Jesus went out to a mountainside to **pray**,
and spent the night **praying** to God.*
Luke 6:12

We had four children in four-and-a-half years. I couldn't go off to a mountain to pray, but I could get them settled and go into the bathroom to pray. We all need quiet times with God, and sometimes we have to be resourceful to get it. Now, decades later, the house is empty, and I can have all the quiet time I want. I cherish it because nothing else fills us up like time with Him, nothing else equips us for our day like time with Him, and nothing else prepares us for what is ahead like time with Him.

Prayer links us to God and invites Him to be part of our lives. Prayer makes it possible to see everything through His lens, instead of ours. Prayer makes us grateful. Whatever stage of life you're in, be resourceful and make time for God.

How resourceful are you in making time for God each day?

PRAYER

Lord Jesus, help me be resourceful in finding time to spend with You because I need You.

November 21

BE A WITNESS

*My **prayer** is not that you take them out of the world
but that you protect them from the evil one.*
John 17:15

You would think Jesus' last night on earth would be a big celebration of all He had accomplished in His three years of public ministry. You would think the disciples would have seen to it. But Jesus knew they didn't understand He was really going to die the next day, so His last night was all about them—and all about us.

John 17 records the most beautiful and comprehensive prayer in the whole Bible as Jesus prays the most fitting prayer for all believers going forward. He asks God not to take us out of the world, but to protect us from the evil one. He wants us to be His witnesses in the world, but Satan will always keep us from it if he can. Let's help God answer Jesus' prayer and be a strong witness for Him in the world.

How are you a witness for Jesus in the world? How are you not?

PRAYER

Lord Jesus, help me be part of God's answer to Your prayer and be a strong witness for You in the world.

❧

TOP PRIORITY

*And [we] will give our attention
to **prayer** and the ministry of the word.*
Acts 6:4

Teaching a weekly women's Bible Study taught me a new thing about prayer. I was totally dependent on God to do it, so I had to pray. There is no greater responsibility than teaching His Word, because eternal lives are at stake, and His Word exposes Satan and his influence in our world. We have to pray for wisdom, knowledge, discernment, and confidence.

All believers are called to be ministers of God's Word, whether you are teaching your toddler, your teenager, a Sunday School class, or in a retirement center, the necessity for prayer is the same. There is no greater responsibility, no greater need, and no greater privilege. God has to do it, and we have to pray He does. Prayer has to be our top priority, so it's His Word and not ours.

Whom are you teaching God's Word to and are you praying before you do?

PRAYER

Lord Jesus, don't let me presume I can teach Your Word without coming to You first. Show me the way.

November 23

SOMEONE IS LISTENING

About midnight Paul and Silas were
praying *and singing hymns to God, and*
the other prisoners were listening to them.
Acts 16:25

P aul and Silas had been beaten and thrown in prison.
They had every right to have a pity party instead of a
revival. But what would that have done for the prisoners?
God knew He could trust Paul and Silas to represent Him
well. He knew He could trust them not to feel sorry for themselves but to see their situation as yet another opportunity
to share the gospel.

Sometimes sharing the gospel means sharing Jesus' suffering. Sometimes it means being jerked out of our comfort zone and stripped of our dignity. Sometimes it means
being with people we don't know and have nothing in
common with—except we are all sinners and we all need
Christ. Speak up! Someone is listening.

Who is listening to you? Are you up for God surprising you
in how and where He wants you to share the gospel?

PRAYER

Lord Jesus, help me be eager to share the gospel wherever
You put me and with whomever You want.

❧

CRUISE CONTROL

The Spirit helps us in our weakness.
*We do not know what we ought to **pray** for,*
but the Spirit himself intercedes for us with
groans that words cannot express.
Romans 8:26

Sometimes our circumstances overwhelm us to the point we don't even know how to pray. I remember a wise woman telling me when that happens to stop praying and start praising. Praising God frees us from the burden and allows the Holy Spirit to take over and pray for us. He knows the problems we are facing, He knows our needs, and He knows how to pray in ways we can't. He is there to help us when we can't help ourselves.

We can compare the Holy Spirit to the cruise control on our car. We can take our foot off the pedal and trust it will keep us going at a safe speed. The Holy Spirit lives in us to take over for us when we are weak—too weak to even pray. Push cruise control and let the Holy Spirit take over.

Next time you feel too weak to pray, will you push cruise control and let the Holy Spirit pray for you? He will.

PRAYER

Lord Jesus, help me allow Your Spirit to pray for me when I am too weak to pray for myself.

❧

A PERFECT THANKSGIVING

*Be joyful in hope, patient in affliction, faithful in **prayer**.*
Romans 12:12

Do you ever wonder how people go through life without Jesus? Paul wondered the same thing after his Damascus Road conversion. Before that experience he thought he had control of his life, and everything was going just as he planned. But then he met Jesus, and it changed him forever. From that point forward, Paul knew what it meant to be joyful in hope, because he knew the risen Lord. He knew what it meant to be patient in affliction, because he suffered for Him. And he knew what it meant to be faithful in prayer, because he needed Him.

The truth is we can't go through life without Jesus. He is the reason for our hope, He is with us in our sufferings, He hears our prayers, and He gives us joy. Jesus makes all the difference. A perfect Thanksgiving, regardless of what day it falls on.

How is Jesus making a difference in your life right now?

PRAYER

Lord Jesus, thank You for being there for me. Help me be joyful in hope, patient in affliction and faithful in prayer.

༢༠

JUST A BREATH AWAY

*And **pray** in the Spirit on all occasions
with all kinds of **prayers** and requests.*
Ephesians 6:18

For Christians, prayer is like breathing. It is necessary for survival. The Holy Spirit makes God accessible to us anytime day or night. He is our traveling companion on our journey of faith. We can cry, call, plead, beg, whisper, or just send Him a quick 'text,' and He is there ready to help. The Holy Spirit links us to God and guarantees our prayers are getting through and being heard.

I am still trying to figure out my car. It has all kinds of 'helps' on it to make driving as easy and safe as possible, and to help me reach my destination. The Holy Spirit does the same for us. He directs us how to pray our way through each day to make life easier and help us reach our destination. Prayer is always just a breath away.

Is prayer as easy as breathing for you, or do you pray only when you are desperate?

PRAYER

Lord Jesus, help me pray in the Spirit on all occasions with all kinds of prayers and requests.

❧

THE PERFECT SOLUTION

*Do not be anxious about anything, but in everything, by **prayer** and petition, with thanksgiving, present your requests to God.*
Philippians 4:6

How do you handle the stress in your life, especially during the holidays? We all have different ways. I love to play tennis; you might love to knit. But God has us covered. He knew our lives would be hard, He knew they would be stressful, and He has provided the perfect solution—Himself. We are to stop stress in its tracks and come to Him, tell Him all about it, thank Him for listening and caring, and then ask Him to help us through it.

My daughter came for dinner tonight, because she was all stressed out, so we prayed. Prayer might not change the situation right away, but it changes us right away, because it relieves us of the responsibility and puts it on God. He is there for us. He is the perfect solution for our stress, any time of the year.

How do you handle stress in your life? How will you handle it now?

PRAYER

Lord Jesus, help me bring my stress to You because You always have the perfect solution.

November 28

❧

THE POWER OF PRAYER

*The **prayer** of a righteous
man is powerful and effective.*
James 5:16

D o you ever wonder what people are thinking when they say, "I'll cross my fingers," "wish you luck," "think good thoughts," or "hope for the best," when you share a personal need with them? What power or source of strength or wisdom are they tapping into? They may have good intentions and mean well, but how does that compare with the power of Almighty God we have at our disposal?

Christians have direct access to the Throne of God because of Jesus. All of His resources are available to us because of Jesus. And we are considered righteous before Him because of Jesus. Therefore, we can approach Him boldly and confidently knowing our simplest most heartfelt prayer will be powerful and effective.

Do you pray trusting God's power, or do you trust your circumstances to chance?

PRAYER

Lord Jesus, help me trust Your power to work in my circumstances.

❧

GOLDEN BOWLS

*They were holding golden bowls full of incense
which are the **prayers** of the saints.*
Revelation 5:8

I don't know about you, but I reserve my most elegant bowls for the things I love the most—precious jewelry, beautiful flowers, yummy food. When John was exiled on the Island of Patmos for his faith, God gave him visions of the future, so we could know where our journey of faith is taking us. God gave him a glimpse of Heaven. In this vision, angels are holding golden bowls filled with our prayers. Can you imagine how many bowls it would take to contain them all? And can you imagine how precious they are to God for keeping them all? It proves how important our prayers are and that we can trust Him. He is keeping a record of our journey, and He will lead us Home. In the meantime, let's keep filling His golden bowls.

Do you realize how precious your prayers are to God?

PRAYER

Lord Jesus, help me realize how precious my prayers are to You and trust You more because they are.

❧

MAKE SURE YOU RSVP

Then a voice came from the throne, saying:
*"**Praise** our God, all you his servants,*
you who fear him, both small and great."
Revelation 19:5

It's only fitting that we end our month on prayer with praise. In this vision of Heaven, John is given a preview of the wedding of the Lamb, a beautiful picture of the intimacy between Jesus and His people. All believers are invited to the elaborate feast that accompanies it, the Wedding Supper of the Lamb to honor Him. We can't even imagine what a celebration and what a feast that will be, with all the people from all nations, languages, races, and walks of life joining together to praise Him and celebrate with Him. What a day that will be! We will thank Jesus for His invitation, and be forever grateful we RSVP'd. You're invited! Make sure you RSVP.

Have you RSVP'd to Jesus' invitation to join Him at His Wedding Supper of the Lamb?

PRAYER

Lord Jesus, thank You for Your invitation. I send a resounding YES!

December

PEACE

❧

Claim God's **peace**
on your journey of faith.

SHALOM

*The Lord turn his face toward
you and give you **peace**.*
Numbers 6:26

As we conclude our journey of faith in the month of December, what better subject to focus on than God's peace? One definition of *peace* is the absence of conflict. But where do we find peace? The world is in constant conflict. In fact, our world has never been less peaceful. Only God can change it, because only God can change the human heart.

God's definition of *peace* is not just the absence of conflict, but a positive state of rightness and well-being. Such peace can only come from Him, because only He can make us right. His peace is peace in the fullest sense of the word. We can't control what's going on in the world, but we can control our reactions. In Hebrew, the word for God's peace is *shalom*. As we continue our journey, shalom!

Do you have God's peace in an ever-changing, always-in-turmoil world? If not, will you ask Him for it?

PRAYER

Lord Jesus, give me Your peace in a very unpeaceful world.

SLEEP WELL

*I will lie down and sleep in **peace**,*
for you alone, O Lord, make me dwell in safety.
Psalm 4:8

D o you long for a good night's sleep? Numerous ads on TV promote better beds, softer pillows, effective medications, and even an app with Bible stories read in a soothing voice guaranteed to put us to sleep. That one sounds good to me, but I know from my own experience that I won't sleep well unless everything is good between me and God. Even then I can toss and turn, but knowing my conscience is clear helps me focus on Him. That makes those sleepless nights times of worship instead of time to worry. His peace will always overshadow our problems, if we claim it and allow it to cover us like a warm blanket. Trust Jesus with your burdens, and let Him put you to sleep.

What do you do when you can't sleep? Will you use the time to worship instead of worry and let Jesus put you to sleep?

PRAYER

Lord Jesus, help me trust You with whatever keeps me awake so I can sleep in Your peace.

December 3

SEEK PEACE

Turn from evil and do good;
*seek **peace** and pursue it.*
Psalm 34:14

Many people today would rather live in constant chaos than peace. They seem to thrive on the adrenalin rush of the crowds seeking to do evil rather than enjoy the peace and satisfaction of doing good. It takes a conscious effort to choose which path we want to be on. It always boils down to two—good and evil. They have been at odds with each other since Satan tempted Adam and Eve in the Garden, and they fell for his lies hook, line, and sinker!

We are confronted with a choice every day—give in to Satan and the evil he perpetuates, or live for Christ and receive the peace He offers. Our screens keep us abreast of all the evil in our world. We have to remember our verse for today and seek peace and pursue it.

What evil influence can you turn away from so you can turn to Christ instead?

PRAYER

Lord Jesus, help me reject evil and do good, so I can enjoy Your peace.

THE PERFECT COMBINATION

*Righteousness and **peace**
kiss each other.*
Psalm 85:10

God only blesses us with His peace when our behavior is right before Him. It makes for a good incentive when we are tempted to tell a lie, join in some gossip, or let our anger get the best of us.

I remember as a child, whenever my siblings and I asked our mom what she wanted for her birthday, her response was always the same—five good kids! It was much easier to make her a card or buy her a gift, but she didn't want something tangible. She wanted good behavior and the peace it would bring. We could pull it off for a day or two, but that never stopped her from asking again—and again. I think if we were to ask God the same question, His answer would be the same—just good kids. Good behavior and peace go together. The perfect combination.

Are you living right before God, so He is blessing you with His peace?

PRAYER

Lord Jesus, help me live right before You, so I have the blessing of Your peace.

December 5

HAVE A GOOD LIFE

*Great **peace** have they who
love your law, and nothing
can make them stumble.*
Psalm 119:165

B oundaries are good. They help us know where we stand. God gave us the Ten Commandments to know where we stand with Him. When we follow them, we are blessed with His approval which always proves itself in His peace. When we reject or ignore them, we are living in disobedience and forfeiting that peace.

Lack of peace is God's way of pulling us back to Him, because He loves us too much to watch us stumble through life. He wants to help us, He wants to guide us, He wants to bless us. He is there for us, and He wants to give us His peace because He knows we are miserable without it. Live inside His boundaries. He wants you to have a good, wholesome, and productive life.

Are you walking with God in obedience or stumbling because of disobedience?

PRAYER

Lord Jesus, help me walk in obedience to You so I won't stumble.

DON'T BE ROBBED

*A heart at **peace** gives life to the body,*
but envy rots the bones.
Proverbs 14:30

The southeast just experienced another devastating hurricane. Homes were obliterated and millions are without water and power. Yet Instead of complaining about what they had lost or begrudging those whose homes were spared, people interviewed on national TV were praising God for their lives. Their response is a powerful example of peace in the midst of unthinkable fear and loss, proving the truth of this proverb that nothing in this world compares with the peace we have in Jesus Christ. It's a waste of time wanting anything less. Don't let envy rob you of the peace Jesus wants to give you, regardless of your circumstances.

Are you allowing envy to rob you of the peace you can have in Jesus?

PRAYER

Lord Jesus, help nothing I do or desire rob me of the peace I can have in You.

December 7

THE LESSON OF A LIFETIME

*Better a dry crust with **peace** and quiet*
than a house full of feasting, with strife.
Proverbs 17:1

The year 2020 taught us many lessons—not the least of which is the importance of the time we spend with our family at home. During the pandemic, our homes became more important to us as the world outside shut down. Home improvement sales soared as we tried to make our homes better and more suitable to our circumstances.

But perhaps the best take-away from the shutdown was the importance of getting along with each other as a family. It brought our hectic schedules to a grinding halt, and we had to adjust to forced time together. We had to create new ways and resurrect old ways of keeping peace and avoiding conflict. The wisdom of this proverb proved true. Peace became a new priority. The lesson of a lifetime.

How did the lessons of last year make your family better this year?

PRAYER

Lord Jesus, after You, our family is most important. Help me make mine a place of peace and not strife.

December 8

A TIME FOR EVERYTHING

A time to love and a time to hate,
a time for war and a time for **peace***.*
Ecclesiastes 3:8

S olomon inherited a prosperous kingdom from his father, King David. He had all the material assets to manage his new responsibility, except one—he lacked the wisdom and maturity necessary to keep the country going in the right direction. So he did the wise thing. He asked God for wisdom, and God gave it to him. Solomon used his gift wisely. His kingdom prospered, He built the Temple in Jerusalem, and in his old age, he wrote Ecclesiastes. Age, experience, and God's wisdom inspired these words that are part of his timeless writing: *A Time for Everything.*

There is a time for everything, and we are wise when we recognize it is from God and ask for His wisdom, like Solomon did, so we do the right thing at the right time.

What season of life are you in and will you claim God's wisdom to guide you?

PRAYER

Lord Jesus, help me ask for Your wisdom in the changing seasons and circumstances of my life.

THE REASON FOR THE SEASON

And he will be called Wonderful Counselor,
*Mighty God, Everlasting Father, Prince of **Peace**.*
Isaiah 9:6

As Christmas is fast approaching and we are in the throes of addressing cards, baking cookies, and wrapping presents, let's not forget that Jesus is the reason for the season! That might be a modern cliché, but it is the timeless truth. Amidst all the glitter and gifts, Jesus is the best gift of all. He is our Wonderful Counselor—with us 24/7 to guide us through this life. He is our Mighty God—sovereign and powerful over everything here on earth. He is our Everlasting Father—who loves us and cares for us like no one else can. And He is our Prince of Peace. There is no peace without Jesus. The prophet Isaiah gave us this preview of Him seven hundred years before He was born. And He is still the reason for the season!

What will you do to make sure Jesus is the reason for your Christmas season?

PRAYER

Lord Jesus, help me make You the center of our family's Christmas season.

December 10

❧

PERFECT PEACE

*You will keep in perfect **peace** him whose
mind is steadfast, because he trusts in you.*
Isaiah 26:3

Who wouldn't like to have a steadfast mind? Think of it! Our minds can be indecisive, wishy-washy, weak, uncertain, and half-hearted. The world we live in and the nightly news we listen to guarantees it. Trying to determine fake news from real news keeps our minds in turmoil and uncertainty. It's hard to know who or what to believe.

But God is there for us, and He wants to give us the peace we all seek. He wants to give us perfect peace. There's only one condition, we have to turn to Him and trust Him. When we do, He blesses us with a steadfast mind—a mind that is firm, resolute, intentional, and determined. Why would we trust anything or anyone else? Only God can give us perfect peace.

Whom or what are you turning to or depending on to give you peace?

PRAYER

Lord Jesus, give me a steadfast mind so I can trust You and experience Your peace.

BEAUTIFUL FEET

How beautiful on the mountains are the feet
*of those who bring good news, who proclaim **peace**,*
who bring good tidings, who proclaim salvation,
who say to Zion, "Your God reigns!"
Isaiah 52:7

I love this verse because I have ugly feet. All the pedicures I can have and the nail polish I can apply doesn't hide the truth: they are still ugly! But God knew how concerned we would be about our feet, so He told us how to make them beautiful—just talk about Him. Tell people about Him. Teach our kids and grandkids about Him. Teach that Sunday school class or that Bible study. Share what He has done with anyone and everyone, because His news is the best good news they will ever hear. Shout His name from the rooftops and the mountaintops. And then look down and see the most beautiful feet you ever saw.

How comfortable are you to tell others about Jesus?

PRAYER

Lord Jesus, help me be bold and confident in my faith so I can tell others about You.

December 12

THE BEST PATH

*The way of **peace** they do not know;*
there is no justice in their paths.
Isaiah 59:8

People determined to live in sin like the path they are on. They don't want to hear about God, because they do not want to be accountable to Him. Isaiah sounded this warning thousands of years ago, and it reverberates down through the ages, because the human condition has not changed.

We are all sinners, and we are helpless to change the direction of our lives apart from Jesus Christ. That's why He tells us we *must* be born again (John 3:3). Only Jesus can change our desires, our motives, our attitudes, and our direction. He sets us on a new path, and He gives what we will never have without Him—peace with Him, peace with ourselves, and justice toward others.

Are you on the best path with Jesus?

PRAYER

Lord Jesus, this is a question between You and me. Help me answer it honestly because I want to be on the best path.

LASTING PEACE

*"**Peace, peace**," they say, when there is no **peace**.*
Jeremiah 6:14

P eople are desperate for peace. Peace marches are taking place in our cities, and yet they aren't even peaceful. We fool ourselves if we think we can manufacture peace apart from God. He is the source of peace and until we recognize Him, honor Him, and trust Him as the Supreme and Sovereign Ruler of the universe, peace will elude us.

And yet, there are people today, just as there were in Jeremiah's day, who tell us we can have peace another way. We think we can march for peace, sign treaties for peace, or make promises for peace, only to have no peace. There will always be people declaring peace, but we will not see real and lasting peace until Jesus Christ returns.

How are you trying to manufacture peace in your life apart from Jesus?

PRAYER

Lord Jesus, help me find my peace in You.

BE BLESSED

*"And in this place I will grant **peace**,"*
declares the Lord Almighty.
Haggai 2:9

H aggai was a prophet in Jerusalem after the Israelites returned from exile in Babylon for their disobedience to God. He encouraged them to learn from their experience and live in obedience instead. Rebuilding their temple would be their first priority to re-establish their relationship with Him. The temple was rebuilt, and the people enjoyed a time of peace.

We can learn from the Israelites. Disobedience always brings God's judgment while obedience brings His blessings. No prideful, willful act of disobedience is worth the peace He gives us when we are putting Him first and living in obedience to Him. He wants to bless us in this place. Be blessed.

How are you living in disobedience to God and forfeiting the peace He wants to give you?

PRAYER

Lord Jesus, help me give up my willful disobedience so my life is blessed with Your peace.

THE BEST IS YET TO COME

*He will proclaim **peace** to the nations.*
His rule will extend from sea to sea and from
the River to the ends of the earth.
Zechariah 9:10

The prophet Zechariah is looking forward to the day we are all looking forward to—the day Jesus returns to this earth to establish a universal kingdom of peace. It's hard for us to imagine, when the world we live in is so unpeaceful. But Jesus is coming to change that. Nations that have fought against each other will lay down their weapons. Division, anarchy, riots, crime, and lawlessness will cease in our cities. People from all backgrounds, races, and cultures will get along. Jesus will show the world what political correctness really is—there won't be any. He will rule the world with fairness and justice for all. And we will know real peace for the first time. The best is yet to come!

How does your life reflect that you are looking forward to Jesus' return?

PRAYER

Lord Jesus, I can't wait for You to return and bring Your peace. Help my life reflect my anticipation.

December 16

WAIT AND SEE

---

*Do not suppose that I have come to bring **peace** to the earth. I did not come to bring **peace**, but a sword.*
Matthew 10:34

Jesus came to bring peace—peace between us and God—and peace between believers. But there will always be conflict between believers and unbelievers, even within the same family. There is a barrier in these relationships, because Jesus is on one side and the devil is on the other. When we understand the reason for the separation, we can stand strong in our convictions and pray. We can pray God's love, power, grace, mercy, and sovereignty overwhelm the unbeliever and draw them to Jesus. And then wait and see what He will do, because He wants everyone to join Him on His side and experience His peace.

What relationship in your life is divided because of your faith in Jesus Christ?

PRAYER

Lord Jesus, help me stand strong in my convictions and pray, and then wait and see what You will do.

WHAT A SIGHT

Glory to God in the highest, and on earth
***peace** to men on whom his favor rests.*
Luke 2:14

Imagine being a lowly shepherd out in the fields around Bethlehem minding your own business and tending your sheep, when suddenly the night sky lights up with multitudes of angels praising God. One of them speaks for the rest and makes this announcement of peace for all the world to hear—and the world has never been the same. Those lowly shepherds aren't so lowly anymore. They are celebrated every year as the first to hear this glorious news that the Savior of the world has come into the world.

Think of it! Jesus chose a teenage virgin for His mother, a humble carpenter as His earthly father, a stable for His make-shift nursery, and a few poor and weary shepherds to announce His arrival. What a sight it must have been as the greatest breaking news of all time reached our planet! And peace became possible.

How are you bringing glory to Jesus this Christmas season?

PRAYER

Lord Jesus, help me spread this greatest news of all time this Christmas and all year.

THINK AGAIN!

*Peace I leave with you; my **peace** I give you.*
I do not give to you as the world gives. Do not let
your hearts be troubled and do not be afraid.
John 14:27

What is troubling you today? What has you most anxious or fearful? Take a moment and reflect on these words Jesus spoke to His disciples when they were terrified of the prospect of His leaving them. His message is emphatic. *Do NOT let your hearts be troubled. Do NOT be afraid because I am NOT leaving you without part of Myself. My peace will be with you. Don't seek or settle for anything less. It is Mine to give you and yours to claim.*

Now think again, what is troubling you today? What are you most fearful of? Give it to Jesus. He will calm your troubled heart, arrest your fears, and give you His peace.

Will you give Jesus your troubles and fears and claim His peace in their place?

PRAYER

Lord Jesus, thank You for taking my troubles and fears so I can have Your peace.

December 19

BE AN OVERCOMER

*I have told you these things so that in me you may have **peace**. In this world you will have trouble. But take heart! I have overcome the world.*
John 16:33

God created the world, but the world was not nice to His Son. Jesus had a rough beginning, lived a humble life, and died a brutal death. He knew all about trouble. He knew how cruel the world could be. He has the perfect credentials to tell us, like He did the disciples, not to let our troubles get us down, but to take heart and keep going.

Jesus overcame His troubles and through Him we can overcome ours, but we do have a choice. He told us these things so we *may* have peace. We can choose to have a pity party and wallow in our misery, or we can come to Him for His peace. It's important we make the right choice, because He also says we *will* have trouble. Let's follow His example and allow His peace to overcome our troubles. Be an overcomer!

Are you choosing to have a pity party over the peace Jesus wants to give you?

PRAYER

Lord Jesus, help me give my stubbornness to You and choose the peace You want to give me.

❦

BE JUSTIFIED

*Therefore, since we have been justified
through faith, we have **peace** with God
through our Lord Jesus Christ.*
Romans 5:1

The basis for our peace with God is justification. *Justification* is a difficult word with a simple meaning: not guilty! In God's court of law, believers are declared not guilty, because we have been to the cross and received the atoning sacrifice for our sin that Jesus died to give us. The theological definition of *justification* is the act by which a sinner is freed through faith from the penalty of sin and is accepted by God as righteous. We give Jesus our sin, He gives us His righteousness, and we can stand boldly before God with a clear conscience and a glorious future. It's the best trade any of us will ever make! Be justified in God's sight.

As we come to the end of our journey of faith, have you made this trade?

PRAYER

Lord Jesus, help me see myself as a sinner in need of Your justification. I want to stand before God in Your righteousness instead of my sin and hear Him say, "Not guilty!"

December 21

LET GOD WIN!

*The mind of sinful man is death, but the mind controlled by the Spirit is life and **peace**.*
Romans 8:6

Before we come to Christ, we live with one spirit, or one nature, in us—our own—which is inerrantly sinful. Our sinful nature controls our mind which controls everything we do. Our sinful nature tells us to reject God and live the way we want to. Our sinful nature is unacceptable to God and will lead to eternal death.

But when we come to Christ, His Holy Spirit moves in and gives us a new nature. Our sinful nature will always be with us and compete with Him for control. It's up to us to let Him win. When we do, we are filled with life and peace, both now and for all eternity. Let God win!

Which nature is controlling your mind today?

PRAYER

Lord Jesus, help me allow Your Spirit to control my mind, so I have Your life and peace.

December 22

❧

TAKE THE HIGH ROAD

If it is possible, as far as it depends on you,
*live at **peace** with everyone.*
Romans 12:18

Jesus wants us to live in peace with others whenever it is possible. Sometimes it is, and sometimes it isn't. But He wants us to make the effort when we can. He wants us to be peacemakers. In fact, it is one of His eight Beatitudes, or blessings, in His Sermon on the Mount (Matthew 5:3-10).

If we listen carefully, we can hear Jesus' voice echoing off the Sea of Galilee where a huge crowd had gathered to hear Him preach. "Blessed are the peacemakers for they shall be called sons of God!" Blessed means to make happy. We are happy when we take the high road and make the effort to bring God's peace to a situation or a relationship. Take the high road!

Whom can you take the high road and make peace with today?

PRAYER

Lord Jesus, thank You for giving me Your peace that makes it possible for me to live at peace with others.

GIVE HIM YOUR BEST

*For God is not a God of disorder but of **peace**.*
1 Corinthians 14:33

Paul is addressing worship in the church in Corinth. He makes the case that God has always told us how we are to worship Him. We wouldn't know otherwise. In the Old Testament, He gave the Israelites specific rules and regulations. Animal sacrifices prepared them for the once-for-all sacrifice Jesus would make centuries later. Festivals and Feast Days brought them together to worship Him as the one true God. The Ark of the Covenant represented His presence with them, and He demanded their utmost reverence and respect.

God didn't want to be worshiped just any old way. He still doesn't. His holiness demands our full and orderly attention. It still does. I wonder what He would think of some of our church services today. He deserves our very best. We have peace when we give it to Him.

Do you give God your best in your worship of Him?

PRAYER

Lord Jesus, help me worship You the way You deserve to be worshiped.

❧

OUR FINAL GUARANTEE

*For he himself is our **peace**.*
Ephesians 2:14

Christmas Eve. The night we celebrate Jesus' birth. Imagine a world without Him. Imagine a world drowning in sin without a Savior to save us. Imagine a world living in darkness with no hope of ever seeing the light. Imagine a world with nothing to look forward to but death. Imagine a world with no chance of ever being reconciled to God. Imagine a world with only one destination—Hell. That's what life would be like without Jesus.

Jesus left the presence of His Father and the glory of Heaven to come down here to change this world and to change us. Love compelled Him, because He wasn't about to let Satan destroy us. Jesus came to assure us he won't. Peace is our final guarantee.

Do you have the peace of Jesus in your heart this Christmas?

PRAYER

Lord Jesus, thank You for coming into this world to bring Your peace. Help me receive it today.

MERRY CHRISTMAS!

*Stand firm then . . . with your feet fitted with the readiness that comes from the gospel of **peace**.*
Ephesians 6:14-15

C hristmas is under attack by the secular world. We see it everywhere. "Happy Holidays" has replaced "Merry Christmas!" Nativity scenes are taken down and schools prohibit traditional Christmas programs, all in an attempt to make it a generic holiday and fair to everyone. But Jesus didn't come to be a part of the world. He came to save the world.

As believers, it will always be our great honor and responsibility to spread His message of salvation. No other religion, no other belief system, no other philosophy can make such a claim. Only Jesus can rescue us from sin and offer us eternal security as a result. Stand firm and be ready to tell people why you celebrate Christmas. It's the best present you can give them—and wish them a Merry Christmas!

How is Jesus included in your Christmas and how are you telling others about Him?

PRAYER

Lord Jesus, it's Your birthday! Help me include You in all I do and be ready to share You with others.

❦

THE PEACE OF GOD

*The **peace** of God, which transcends all
understanding, will guard your hearts and
your minds in Christ Jesus.*
Philippians 4:7

O ur human minds cannot comprehend the totality of
God. We cannot begin to understand the magnitude
of His love and care, His grace and mercy, His forgiveness
and faithfulness. We can't really wrap our heads around
a God who pours Himself into us the way He does. And it
boggles our mind to think that Jesus wanted to enter our
world as a helpless baby when He is coming again as King.

That's the beauty of God's peace—it goes way beyond
our ability to understand. But we know when we experience it. We know it when our hearts are broken, and our
hopes are dashed. We know it when we are consumed
with worry and fear and yet—His peace surpasses it all.

How are you experiencing God's peace today?

PRAYER

Lord Jesus, thank You that Your peace transcends all understanding and yet it's mine.

December 27

ALL FOR US
---

*For God was pleased to have all his fullness dwell
in him, and through him to reconcile to himself all
things, whether things on earth or things in heaven, by
making* **peace** *through his blood, shed on the cross.*
Colossians 1:19-20

God the Father, Jesus the Son, and the Holy Spirit work in perfect tandem with each other. They worked together creating our universe, they worked together planning our salvation, and they are working together to bring all of creation back to the place it was before sin entered the human race and threatened to annihilate us.

God didn't create us to be annihilated, so He came in human form, in the Person of Jesus to make things right again. He came to take our sin so we could be reconciled to a Holy God. He came to make peace between us. He did it all for us, because to Him, we are worth it.

Do you know your own worth to God?

PRAYER

Lord Jesus, thank You for loving me so much that You sent Jesus to die for me so I can have peace with You.

❧

GIVE HIM YOUR ALL

*May God himself, the God of **peace**,*
sanctify you through and through.
1 Thessalonians 5:23

When my grandson was little, he complained of having pain in his chest. Of course, my daughter was concerned so she asked him about it, and his explanation was, "I think I just have too much Jesus in my heart!" Oh, that we could have too much Jesus! Oh, that He could have all of us instead of just a part of us. Think what He could do if He did. And think what we are forfeiting when He doesn't.

We are forfeiting Jesus' right to reign in our life. We are forfeiting the blessing of obedience. We are forfeiting moving forward in our journey of faith and being sanctified through and through. We are forfeiting His pleasure. And we our forfeiting the peace He wants to give us. Give Jesus your whole heart. Give Him your all!

How much of you does Jesus have?

PRAYER

Lord Jesus, help me give You my entire self so You can make me all You want me to be.

December 29

GIVE HIM THE GLORY
---

*May the God of **peace** . . . equip you*
with everything good for doing his will.
Hebrews 13:20-21

When God calls us to do a work for Him, He equips us to do it. Otherwise, it's our idea, our motives, our energy, and our strength all working for our own benefit. We may have good intentions and think we are doing the right thing, but unless we are listening to Him and surrendering to His will over our will, our works are self-serving. I have seen this principle work in my life—when He called me to lead my first small group, when He called me to teach, and later, when He called me to write. With each experience, He was calling me out of my comfort zone so I could not depend on myself, but only on Him. I learned it's best to just say, "Yes," and then watch Him do it. You will get the peace and He gets the glory, as He should. Give Him the glory!

What is God calling you to do that is out of your comfort zone?

PRAYER

Lord Jesus, help me trust Your will over my own so I depend on You.

REAP A HARVEST

Peacemakers *who sow in* ***peace***
raise a harvest of righteousness.
James 3:18

G od calls us to be peacemakers in a world that is any-thing but peaceful, because He is the God of peace. He gives us His wisdom to handle problems and situations correctly, so we get the right result. He calls us to be peace-loving, considerate, submissive, full of mercy and good fruit, impartial and sincere (James 3:17). This is His way and as His followers, it should be our way.

Unfortunately, we see conflict, strife, hatred, anger, and violence hijack our attempts at peace in our world, our country, our cities, our communities, our schools, and our homes. But these responses are from Satan, not God. God does not call us to turn our back on evil but to face evil His way. Only His way produces the right result. Reap a harvest!

Are you confronting the evil in your life God's way or your way?

PRAYER

Lord Jesus, help me confront evil Your way, because only Your way produces the right result.

IT'S A GREAT JOURNEY!
LOOK FORWARD

---

*So then, dear friends, since you are looking forward to this [the Lord's return] make every effort to be found spotless, blameless and at **peace** with him.*
2 Peter 3:14

As we come to the end of our journey of faith, it's a good time to evaluate how far we have come and where we want to be. As for me, I don't want just a part of God, I want all of Him. I want Him to infuse my body, mind, and spirit with His presence. I want Him to permeate every cell of my being. I want Him to have His way with me. I want Him to use me up before I die. I want to stand before Him as His forgiven child and hear Him say, "Well done, good and faithful servant! . . . Come and share your master's happiness (Matthew 25:21)!"

Only because of Jesus and His atoning sacrifice on our behalf can we ever hope to have such a glorious ending to our journey here on earth. But thanks to Him, we can! Look forward, thank Jesus as you go, and you will end up where you want to be.

As we come to the end of our journey together, where are you in your own journey of faith?

PRAYER

Lord Jesus, thank You for this journey with You. Help me continue on with You until You take me home.

The Lord bless you and keep you; the Lord make his face shine upon you and be gracious to you; the Lord turn his face toward you and give you **peace.**
Numbers 6:24-26

ACKNOWLEDGMENTS

When God asks us to do something for Him, He gives us the desire, the time, the energy, the focus, and the support we need to get it done. This 'assignment' was no different. In fact, He supplied all I needed in record time. I want to thank my daughter, Jennifer, for your encouragement to write a devotional and your help with the title and cover design. I want to thank my family for always cheering me on. I want to thank Debbie Austin for your incredible commitment and expertise. I could not have done this without you!! I want to thank my readers, Patti Smith, Carol Ferrarini, and Rita Hagmeyer. Most of all, I want to thank You, Lord Jesus, for giving me this privilege. It is for Your honor and glory until You return.

OTHER BOOKS BY THE AUTHOR

Waiting His Return
Claiming Our Inheritance
Seeking Safety in a Scary World

CPSIA information can be obtained
at www.ICGtesting.com
Printed in the USA
FSHW020459181220
77001FS